# BIPLANE

ALSO BY RICHARD BACH

*Stranger to the Ground*
*Nothing by Chance*
*Jonathan Livingston Seagull*
*A Gift of Wings*
*Illusions: The Adventures of a Reluctant Messiah*
*There's No Such Place as Far Away*

# BIPLANE

## RICHARD BACH

*Prelude by Ray Bradbury*

*Photographs by Paul E. Hansen and Richard Bach*

AN ELEANOR FRIEDE BOOK

**MACMILLAN PUBLISHING COMPANY**
NEW YORK

**COLLIER MACMILLAN PUBLISHERS**
LONDON

Macmillan Publishing Company
866 Third Avenue, New York, N.Y. 10022
Collier Macmillan Canada, Inc.

---

Library of Congress Cataloging in Publication Data

Bach, Richard.
Biplane.

Reprint. Originally published: New York: Harper &
Row, c1966.
1. Bach, Richard.   2. Biplanes—Piloting.
3. Air pilots—United States—Biography.   I. Title.
[TL540.B27A26  1983]     629.13'092'4 [B]   83-8001
ISBN 0-02-504670-5

---

10  9  8  7  6  5  4  3  2  1

Printed in the United States of America

TO MY WIFE, WHOM I MET BY THE WING OF A
BIPLANE LANDED IN AN ARIZONA WHEATFIELD,
LATE IN THE EVENING OF 1929

# A PRELUDE TO BACH

DICK BACH couldn't write a book about flying if he tried. And that, son, is a compliment.

If by "flying" we mean a mere manual of technical plans and exercises, how to take off and land, repair a motor, or restring your 1917 piano-wire harp, it is obvious from the first page of this book on that that is not what we are going to get from the very young Mr. Bach.

If on the other hand we intend to ventilate our knowledge, go up with Icarus, come down with Montgolfier and re-ascend with the Wrights, thoroughly aerated and highly exhilarated, then of course we must put ourselves in Dick Bach's farmboy Tom Swift hands. He does not "fly" just as his great-great-great grandfather Johann Sebastian Bach did not "write music": he *exhaled* it.

I am an idea—not a descriptive—writer. But I cannot resist describing Dick Bach to you. He is tall and angular and kind of slopes himself through your door, like Gulliver entering the house of a Lilliputian. He might have just come in off the plowfield. That makes sense, for probably he just emergency-landed his biplane in your north quarter and on his way across to your friendly light he could be expected to have pitched in and helped with the harvest.

He is a great big lunk of an American boy, that same tinkerer and rowboat mechanic we have seen bean-sprouting up by the light of the Industrial Revolution in basements and attics across America since locomotives first dragon-scared the Red Indians and San Juan Teddy dug that Canal singlehanded.

Dick Bach is all the clichés you ever heard about fresh apple pie and the Lafayette Escadrille (lately he has grown a most unlikely blond fairly English mustache).

Look in any old war memorial and you will see his face gazing back at you with proud innocence out of a thousand faded photos. He is so common as to be uncommon. If pictures had been snapped two thousand years ago you would have seen that same fair-reckoning smile and slope-gawked attitude behind Caesar on his way into and out of Britain.

He was never Daedalus, nor was he Icarus: they were special in another way. But he was one of those who saw Daedalus try and Icarus fail, and decided to do it himself, no matter what. So his time-traveling doppelgänger has been leaping off aqueducts and startling Chinese mandarins with bamboo butterfly wings or falling off cowbarns with bumbershoots for something like thirty centuries. Some were runtier than our present Dick Bach of course, but all had that same noon-sunshine apple smile that looks at Doom and says I'll Live Forever.

We despair of him, we weep for him, but finally we laugh with all the Richard Bachs down history who, like grand Stubb in *Moby Dick* knew that a laugh was the best answer to everything.

Here then is Dick Bach's own dear book not about flying but soaring, a feat not of machines but imagination.

Great-great-great grandpa wrote the music. Now here's an offspring to lift simple words.

Perhaps the boy does not fly as high as the old man. Perhaps. But, just look—he is up there.

RAY BRADBURY

*May 17, 1965*

# BIPLANE

# 1

IT IS LIKE OPENING NIGHT on a new way of living, only it is opening day, and instead of velvet curtains drawing majestically aside there are hangar doors of corrugated tin, rumbling and scraping in concrete tracks and being more stubborn than majestic. Inside the hangar, wet still with darkness and with two wide pools of dark underwing and evaporating as the tall doors slide, the new way of living. An antique biplane.

I have arrived to do business, to trade. As simple as that. A simple old airplane trade, done every day. No slightest need to feel unsure.

Still, a crowd of misgivings rush toward me from the hangar. This is an old airplane. No matter how you look at it, this airplane was built in 1929 and this is today and if you're going to get the thing home to California you've got to fly it over twenty-seven hundred miles of America.

It is a handsome airplane, though. Dark red and dark yellow, an old barnstormer of a biplane, with great tall wheels, two open cockpits and a precise tictactoe of wires between the wings.

For shame. You have a fine airplane this moment. Have you forgotten the hours and the work and the money you poured into the rebuilding of the airplane you already own? That was only a year ago! A completely rebuilt 1946 Fairchild 24, as good as brand new! Better than brand new; you know every rib and frame and engine cylinder of the Fairchild, and you know that they're perfect. Can you say as much for this biplane? How do you know that ribs aren't broken beneath that fabric, or wingspars cracked?

How many thousand miles have you flown the Fairchild? Thousands over the Northeast, from that day you rolled her out of the hangar in Colt's Neck, New Jersey. Then from Colt's Neck more thousands to Los Angeles, wife and children seeing the country at first hand as we moved to a new home. Have you forgotten that flight and the airplane that brought your country alive in rivers coursing and great craggy mountains and wheat tassels in the sun? You built this airplane so no weather could stop it, with full flight instruments and dual radios for communication and navigation and a closed cabin to keep out the wind and rain. And now this airplane has flown you across more thousands of miles, from Los Angeles to this little land of Lumberton, North Carolina.

This is good biplane country. March in Lumberton is like June is like August. But the way home is a different land. Remember the frozen lakes in Arizona, three days ago? The snow in Albuquerque? That's no place for an open-cockpit biplane! The biplane is in her proper place this moment. In Lumberton, with tobacco fields green about her airport, with other antique airplanes sheltered nearby, with her gentle

[4]

owner taking time from his law practice to tend to her needs.

This biplane is not your airplane, your *kind* of airplane, even. She belongs and she should belong to Evander M. Britt, of Britt and Britt, attorneys at law. A man who loves old airplanes, with the time to come down and take care of their needs. He has no wild schemes, he hasn't the faintest desire to fly this airplane across the country. He knows his airplane and what it can do and what it can't do. Come to your senses. Just fly home in the Fairchild and forget this folly. His advertisement for a trade should find him his coveted low-wing Aeronca, and from someplace just down the road, not a brand new Fairchild 24 from Los Angeles, California. The biplane doesn't even have a radio!

It is true. If I make this trade, I will be trading the known for the unknown. On the other side stands only one argument, the biplane itself. Without logic, without knowledge, without certainty. I haven't the right to take it from Mr. Britt. Secretary to the local chapter of the Antique Airplane Association, he should have a biplane. He needs a biplane. He is out of his mind to trade this way. This machine is his mark of belonging to an honored few.

But Evander Britt is a grown man and he knows what he is doing and I don't care why he wants the Fairchild or how much money I've put in the rebuilding or how far I've flown in it. I only know that I want that biplane. I want it because I want to travel through time and I want to fly a difficult airplane and I want to feel the wind when I fly and I want people to look, to see, to know that glory still exists. I want to be part of something big and glorious.

This can be a fair trade only because each airplane is worth the same amount of money. Money aside, the two airplanes have absolutely nothing in common. And the biplane? I want it because I want it. I have brought sleeping bag and silk scarf for a biplane voyage home. My decision is made, and now, touching a dark wingtip, nothing can change it.

"Let's roll 'er out on the grass," Evander Britt says. "You can pull on that outboard wing strut, down near the bottom. . . ."

In the sunlight, the darks of red and yellow go bright scarlet and blazing bright flame to become a glowing sunrise-biplane in four separate wing panels of cloth and wood and an engine of five black cylinders. Thirty-five years old, and this hangar could be the factory, and this air, 1929. I wonder if airplanes don't think of us as dogs and cats; for every year they age, we age fifteen or twenty. And as our pets share our household, so do we in turn share with airplanes the changing drifting sweeping household of the sky.

". . . not really so hard to start, but you have to get the right combination. About four shots of prime, pull the prop through five or six times . . ."

It is all strange and different, this cockpit. A deep leather-trimmed wood-and-fabric hole, cables and wires skimming the wooden floorboards, three knobbed stalks of engine controls to the left, a fuel valve and more engine controls forward, six basic engine and flight instruments on a tiny black-painted instrument panel. No radio.

A four-piece windscreen, low in front of my eyes. If it rains now, this whole thing is going to fill with water.

"Give it a couple of slow pumps with the throttle."

"One . . . two. OK." Funny. You never hear of cockpits filling up with water, but what happens when it rains on one of these things?

"One more shot of prime, and make the switches hot."

Click-click on the instrument panel.

"CONTACT! And brakes."

One quick downward swing of the shining propeller and

[6]

the engine is very suddenly running, catching its breath and choking and coughing hoarse in the morning chill. Silence runs terrified before it and hides in the far corners of the forests around. Clouds of blue smoke wreathe for a second and are whipped away and the silver blade becomes nothing more than a great wide fan, and it blows air back over me like a giant blowing on a dandelion and the sound of it over the engine sound is a deep westwind in the pines.

I can't see a thing ahead but airplane; a two-passenger front cockpit and a wide cowling and a silver blur that is the propeller. I let go the brakes and look out over the side of the cockpit into the big fan-wind giant-wind and touch the throttle forward. The propeller blur goes thinner and faster and the engine-sound goes deeper, all the while hollow and resonant, as though it were growling and roaring at the bottom of a thousand-gallon drum, lined in mirrors.

The old tall wheels begin to roll along the grass. The old grass, under the old wind, and bright old wings of another year and of this year, bound solidly together with angled old wires and forward-tilting old struts of wood, all a painted butterfly above the chill Carolina grass. Pressing on the rudder pedals, I swing the nose slowly from one side to the other as we roll, making sure that the blind way ahead is clear.

What a very long way has come the dream of flight since 1929. None of the haughty proud businesslike mien of the modern airplane hinted here. None of it. Just a slow leisurely taxi, with the constant S-turns to see ahead, pausing to sniff the breeze and inspect a flower in the grass and to listen to the sound of our engine. A quiet-seeming old biplane. Seeming, though, only seeming.

I have heard about these old airplanes, heard stories aplenty. Unreliable, these machines. You've always got to be ready for that engine to stop running. Quit on takeoff, usually, just when you need 'em most. And there's nothing you can do about it, that's just the way they are. If you do make it through the takeoff, look out for those old ones once they're in the air. Slow up just a little too much, boy, and they'll jerk the rug right out from under you and send you down in a spin. Like as not, you won't be able to recover from the spin, either. They'll just wrap up tighter and tighter and all you can do is bail out. Not too strange or unusual for the whole engine to fall out, sometimes. You just can't tell. That old metal in those old engine mounts is all crystallized by now, and one day SNAP and there you are falling backward out of the sky. And the wood in these airplanes, look out for that old wood. Rotted clean through, more than likely. Hit a little bump in the air, a little gust of wind, and there goes one of your wings folding and fluttering away, or worse, folding back over the cockpit so that you can't even bail out. But worst of all are the landings. Biplanes have that narrow landing gear and not much rudder to work with; they'll get away from you before you can blink your eyes and suddenly you're rolling along the runway in a big ball of wires and splinters and shredded old fabric. Just plain vicious and that's the only word for 'em. Vicious.

But this airplane seems docile and as trim as a young lady earnestly seeking to make a good impression upon the world. Listen to that engine tick over. Smooth as a tuned racing engine, not a single cylinder left out of the song. "Unreliable," indeed.

A quick engine runup here on the grass before takeoff. Controls all free and working properly, oil pressure and temperature pointing as they should. Fuel valve is on, mixture is rich, all the levers are where they belong. Spark advance lever, even, and a booster magneto coil. Those haven't been built into airplanes for the last thirty years.

All right, airplane, let us see how you can fly. A discreet nudge on the throttle, a touch of left rudder to swing the nose around into the wind, facing a broad expanse of tall moist airport grass. Someone should have stamped out those rumors long ago.

Chinstrap fastened on leather helmet, dark goggles lowered.

Throttle coming full forward, and the giant blows hard twisting sound and fanned exhaust upon me. Certainly aren't very quiet, these engines.

Push forward on the control stick and instantly the tail is flying. Built for little grass fields, the biplanes. Weren't many airports around in 1929. That's why the big wheels, too. Roll over the ruts in a pasture, a racetrack, a country road. Built for shortfield takeoffs, because that's where the passengers were, short fields were where you made your money.

Grass fades into a green felt blur, and the biplane is already light on her wheels.

And suddenly the ground is no more. Smooth into the sky the bright wings climb, the engine thunders in its hollow drum, the tall wheels, still spinning, are lifted. Listen to that! The wind in the wires! And now it's here all around me. It hasn't gone at all. It isn't lost in dusty yellow books with dusty browning photographs. It is here this instant, the taste of it all. That screaming by my ears and that whipping of my scarf—the wind! It's here for me now just as it was here for the first pilots, that same wind that carried their megaphoned words across the pastures of Illinois and the meadows of Iowa and the picnic grounds of Pennsylvania and the beaches of Florida. *"Five dollars, folks, for five minutes. Five minutes with the summer clouds, five minutes in the land of the angels. See your town from the air. You there, sir, how about taking the little lady for a joyride? Absolutely safe, perfectly harmless. Feel that fresh wind that blows where only birds and airplanes fly.*" The same wind drumming on the same fabric and singing through the same wires and smashing into the same engine cylinders and sliced by the same sharp bright propeller and stirred and roiled by the same passage of the same machine that roiled it so many years ago.

If the wind and the sun and the mountains over the horizon do not change, a year that we make up in our heads and on our paper calendars is nothing. The farmhouse, there below. How can I tell that it is a farmhouse of today and not a farmhouse of 1931?

There's a modern car in the driveway. That's the only way I can tell the passing of time. It isn't the calendar makers who give us our time and our modern days, but the designers of automobiles and dishwashers and television sets and the current trends in fashion. Without a new car, then, time stands still. Find an old airplane and with a few pumps of prime and the swing of a shining propeller you can push time around as you will, mold it into a finer shape, give its features a more pleasant countenance. An escape machine, this. Climb in the cockpit and move the levers and turn the valves and start the engine and lift from the grass into the great unchanging ocean of air and you are master of your own time.

The personality of the biplane filters back to me as we fly. Elevator trim has to be almost full down to keep the nose from climbing when I take my hand from the control stick. Aileron forces are heavy, rudder and elevator forces are light. In a climb, I can push the throttle full forward and get no more than 1750 revolutions per minute from the shining propeller. The horizon is balanced, in level flight, just atop the Number Two and Five cylinder heads. The airplane stalls

gently, and before it stalls there is a tapping in the stick, a warning that the nose is about to drop slowly down, even with the control stick pulled back. There's nothing at all vicious about this airplane. Windy, of course, when you move your head from behind the glass windscreen, and not so quiet as modern airplanes. The wind goes quiet when the airplane is near its stalling speed; it shrieks warnings if it flies too fast. There is a great deal of airplane flying out ahead of the pilot. The forward windscreen clouds over with oil film and rocker-box grease after an hour in the air. When the throttle has been back for a moment, the engine misfires and chokes as it comes forward again. Certainly not a difficult airplane to fly. Certainly not a vicious one.

A circle over the airport now, with its great runways lying white ribbons in the grass. The most difficult time, they say, is the landing. I must look over the field carefully and make sure the runway is clear. When I am ready to land, that big nose will block the view ahead and I can only trust that nothing will wander into my path until I can slow down and begin S-turning to see. There, the field that I will land upon, the grass next to the runway. Away over to the left, the gasoline pumps and a little cluster of people watching.

We slide down a long invisible ramp in the sky, down past two giant poplar trees guarding the approach to the runway. The biplane flies so slowly that there is time to watch the poplars and see how their leaves flutter silver in the wind. Then I look out to the side as the runway appears below, look out to the side and judge the height, gage the height of tall wheels above the grass, and with a shudder the stall and the airplane is down and rolling left-rudder right-rudder keep it straight beside the runway don't let it get away from you right-rudder now, just a touch of right rudder. And that's all there is to it. Simple as can be.

Another takeoff, another landing, another bit of knowing tucked away. Somehow, taxiing to the hangar, I'm surprised that it should be so easy to demolish the stories and the grim warnings.

"Evander Britt, you just made a deal."

The trade is completed in a day, with only an occasional rustle in the forest that shows where a misgiving lurks.

I am owner of a 1929 Detroit-Ryan Speedster, model Parks P-2A.

Goodbye, Fairchild. We have flown many hours and learned many things together. Of instruments humming and the things that happen when they cease to hum, of riding invisible radio beams over Pennsylvania and Illinois and Nebraska and Utah and California, of landings at international airports with jetliners close behind and on beaches with only a gull or a sandpiper to hurry us along. But now there is more to learn, and different problems.

The hangar doors that had opened on a new way of life close now on an old one. Into the front cockpit of the Parks go the sleeping bag and sandwiches and the jug of water, cans of sixty-weight oil and cockpit covers and C-26 spark plugs, tools and tape and a coil of soft wire.

Fill the gas tank to its five-hour brim; a last handshake from Evander Britt. From those who stand near and know where I plan to fly, a few faint words.

"Good luck."

"Take it easy, now."

"You be careful, hear?"

A newspaper reporter is interested to find that the biplane is seven years older than its pilot.

Engine started, muttering softly at the bottom of its drum, I buckle into the unfamiliar parachute harness, fasten the safety belt, and jounce slowly over the grass, fanning it back behind me, moving into position for takeoff.

It is one of those times when there is no doubt that a moment is an important moment, one that will be remembered. In that moment, the old throttle goes forward under

[13]

my glove and the first second of a journey begins. The technical details are here, and crowding about: rpm at 1750, oil pressure at 70 psi, oil temperature at 100 degrees F. The other details are here too, and I am ready to learn again: I can't see a *thing* ahead of this airplane when it is on the ground; look how far forward the throttle will move without gaining another revolution from the engine; this is going to be a long and windy journey; note the grassblades growing at the edge of the runway; how quickly the tail is flying and we can skim the ground on the main wheels only. And we're off. A constant thunder and beating twisting wind about me, but I can hear it all as they are hearing it, on the ground: a tiny hum increasing, for a quick second loud and powerful overhead, then dwindling on down the scale to end in a tiny old biplane quiet against the sky.

## 2

As LONG as I'm so few miles from the Atlantic, I'll fly east to the ocean. Make it a more fitting triumph to have flown literally from one coast to the other; from sea, as it were, to shining sea.

We are aloft, and heading east as the sun grows into a cool setting fireball behind. The shine is gone from the railroad tracks, and shadows have washed together into a dark protecting coat for the ground. I am in daylight still, but that is night seeping up out of the ground and my new old airplane has no lights. Barely airborne, it is time to land.

Five minutes away, down and to our right, a field. A pasture. It is a quarter mile long, with only a single row of trees to make the landing approach an interesting problem. We circle the field three times, the biplane and I, watching closely for ruts and holes and tree stumps and hidden ditches.

And in the circling and the watching, the quarter mile of land changes from anonymous old pasture to *my* pasture; my field, my home for the night, my airport. A few minutes ago this land was nothing, now it is my home. I know that I shall have to land well to the left, paralleling the dirt road, avoiding a jackstraw pile of pine logs near the forest.

For the briefest of moments, a frightened voice. What the devil am I doing here, sitting in a wild old biplane with the sun gone down, circling a pasture with intent to land and a good chance of overlooking one felled tree in the dark grass and adding another twenty-three hundred pounds of kindling to the pile of jackstraws? One last cautious pass. The field looks short, and it looks wet, too. But I am committed to land, short or not, wet or not, kindling or not.

Eighty miles per hour and whistling down over the row of trees. One brief sideslip to lose the last of my altitude, black grass blurring by, the pile of giant logs that were jackstraws a moment ago, and in the last second the world forward is blanked in the long wide nose of my new airplane. For better or . . . for . . . worse. The wheels . . . SLAM down. Instant geysers of high-pressure mud swallow the airplane in flying spray and I fight, I just hang on and fight to keep her straight it takes forever to stop we should be stopped by now and we're just barely beginning to slow and the mud is still roaring up from the wheels and I can feel it wet on my face and the world goes dim as it sprays my goggles and we should be stopped by n . . . BAM! what was that the tail, something has snapped in the tail and HANG ON! We finish our mud-landing with a hard wrench to the right, with a great sheet of liquid brown thrown in a tenth second to be a solid storm of mud over airplane and grass for a hundred feet around. We slide to a stop with our tall wheels four inches down in the sodden ground. Switches off and the engine stops and we are forlorn and unmoving, wrapped in a blanket of deepest silence.

Across the field, a bird chirps, one time.

What a landing. Something is broken, for the Parks is twisted, her nose high in the air. So this is what it was like in the old days of flying. A pilot was on his own. If I would live the old days, I must be on my own.

It is clear, in a moment, that nothing will happen and nothing will move unless I make it happen and unless I make it move. We will sit together, the biplane and I, to freeze into mud and all eternity unless I break this silence and move around and find out what damage I have done.

So, while night oozes up out of the mud, I stir and climb over the side of my cockpit to step squishing down and look fearfully upon the tailwheel. It does not look good. Only the tip of the wheel shows round beneath the fuselage, and I am certain that the axle has been smashed and twisted beyond any hope of repair.

But, lying in the mud, pointing a flashlight, I discover that it is not so, that only a small shock cord has broken, allowing the wheel to fold backward. The cord replaced by a length of nylon rope from my front-cockpit supply depot, the wheel rotates down once again into position, ready for other fields to conquer. The work takes ten minutes.

So this is how it was. A pilot handled his own problems as they came, and he went without help wherever he felt like going.

In modern aviation there is a runway for every man, and scores of people earn their living by helping the pilot in need. And mind your conduct, pilot, when the control tower is watching.

What would they have thought, those pilots who barnstormed alone in the Parks and her sisters across the meadows and the early years of flight? Perhaps they would have seen how wonderful it all is today, at the big airports. But perhaps, too, they would have shaken their heads a bit sadly and flown back into the days when they are free and on their own.

Here, in my muddy pasture, I have followed them. This is a barnstormer's field. No control tower or runway here, no fuel-and-oil service, no follow-me truck to tell me where to park. There is not a trace of the present, there is not a hint of time in the air. If I wish, I can find reference in the papers and cards I carry to years labeled 1936 and 1945 and 1954 and May, 1964. And I can burn them all. I can burn them and squash their ashes down into this black mud and press more mud over them, and there I would be, all alone, way out in the middle of now.

Darkness gathers full about us, and I spread my waterproof cockpit cover on the ground beneath the left wing, and the sleeping bag upon the cover, where it will be dry. The only sounds in the whole field, quarter mile long and rimmed in uncut forest, are the sound of a sleeping bag straightened over a canvas cockpit cover and a sound of cold chicken sandwiches unwrapped.

Stretched out beneath the wing of my airplane, I sleep, but wake later in the cold of the night. Above me the sky is moving its fresh cold dark silent way to its own secret horizons. I have watched the sky for hours uncounted and followed it, and crossed horizons with it, and still have not begun to tire. The everchanging, fascinating sky. The airplane, of course, is the key. It makes the sky accessible. As astronomy without a telescope can be uninteresting, so the sky without an airplane. One can watch only so much before he is sated, but when he can participate, when he can move himself through the halls of cloud in the day and travel from star to star in the night, then he can watch with knowing, and does not have to imagine what it would be like to walk those halls and those stars. With an airplane, he can learn to know the sky as an old friend, and to smile when he sees it. No prodding the memory nor need to keep reminders. A glance through a window, a walk along a crowded or along a secluded street, at noon or at midnight. The sky of now is always here, moving; and we, watching, share a part of its secret.

I rest, tonight, partly beneath a white-flour moon and partly beneath a wing of wooden ribs that carries struts and wires to support another wing of wooden ribs above it. This is not happening years ago, I rest here now. The barnstormers? They live with the same moon and the same stars. Their time has not gone, it is still about us.

I wonder about my new biplane. She has spent many calendars safe in a silent hangar, and has been cared for patiently, and rarely flown. The rain did not touch her, nor the sun, nor the wind. And here she is in the mud of a cold night field, sheathed in dirt and water mixed, with dew beading on her wings. Around her no black hangar air, but the sky and stars. Knowing where she is, Evander Britt would wince and turn away. The last remaining Detroit-Parks P-2A flying, the very last, priceless; and tonight, you say, in the MUD?

I have to smile. For I truly think, with no need for guile, that she is happier here. For fields and mud she was built, with fields and mud and nights under the stars in mind she was set from designer's pen to paper. Designed to make her living flying passengers on joyrides from pastures and crossroads, from green-summer county fairs and in rainbow air circuses traveling, traveling. She was designed to be flown.

[19]

The pages of the aircraft logbook, buried now under tool kit and tiedown ropes, are a document of flight, a memory in ruled paper.

"DATE: *May 14, '32*, DURATION OF FLIGHT: *10 min.* NUMBER OF PASSENGERS: *2*." Page after page of five-minute and ten-minute flights, just time for one takeoff, one circle of the field, one landing. Occasionally, in the REMARKS column: "*Total passengers carried to date—810.*" A few pages further; "*Total passengers—975.*" Between these, the column makes minor reference that all landings were not smooth. "*Propeller removed and straightened.*" "*Wingtip repaired.*" "*Tailwheel replaced.*" In September, 1939: "*Passengers—1,233,*" and the next entry: "*Aircraft prepared for storage.*"

If he had not been able to sell the airplane soon, Evander Britt had said, he was going to give her to the National Air Museum, the last aircraft of her type, and a symbol of her time.

Which would you choose, airplane, polished linoleum floors and a life secure behind purple-velvet rope, or the insecurities of mud and moonlight, of bent propellers and wingtips for repair?

A good question for the pilot, too. There can be the security of polished floors and velvet ropes for him, too. No need to be thundering about the countryside, to be tackling highly improbable odds, when he can be forever safe behind a desk. There is only one sacrifice to be made for that security. To be safe he has only to sacrifice living. In safety there are no fears to conquer, no obstacles to overcome, no wild screaming dangers stalking behind the fence of our mistakes. If we wish, velvet ropes, and a single word on the wall: "Silence."

A mist has risen from the damp earth of the field, and under the moon it is a field of spun glass glowing. What is this like?

To what does it compare? I consider for a long time, to discover that it compares to nothing I have ever known. An airplane teaches many things, but always before I have learned in the air, while flying. When the airplane was on the ground, the lesson was over. But tonight, in a nameless field in North Carolina, the airplane huge above me, casting a quiet black shadow across my sleeping bag, I am still learning. Will I never stop learning from airplanes? How can there be room in tomorrow for still another lesson?

The biplane stands serene and unmoving. She seems very sure that there will be room for a lesson tomorrow.

# 3

Adventures begin with the sun. By the time the mist is gone, and the mud dry on the wings, the biplane and I begin our first full day together. The only sounds in the field are the unusual ones of cylinders 1–3–5–2–4 slowly, over and again while the bright blade flickers around.

I pace the field in front of the plane, moving blown tree branches and occasional stones aside, marking the holes that could give difficulty. This first part of the takeoff is critical, before the weight has gone from the wheels into the wings.

The 1–3–5–2–4 comes fainter and fainter as I pace, a soft sewing machine stitching quietly away to itself. If someone wanted, he could dash to the biplane, push the throttle forward, and be gone. I know that the field is deserted, but still I am glad to return and work closer to the biplane.

Sleeping bag stowed in its tight fluffy cylinder and strapped in the front cockpit, giant fan-wind whirring past once again to establish a pattern of familiar, we are ready to say goodbye to a field that has been friend and tutor.

The thought flag comes down, checkered, and a single word: Go. Center of a roaring hemisphere of 1–3–5–2–4 round and round 1750 times a minute, moving slowly at first on heavy wheels, jouncing. Then faster. Then skipping from peak to tiny peak. Splashing mud in the first second, then spattering it, then spraying it hard, then skimming it, then leaving it smooth and untouched, casting down a shuddering black shadow.

Goodbye, field.

A railroad track points east, and so does the nose of the Parks. For the decision to fly from coast to coast, for the poor human frailty of wanting to tie things in neat packages with colorful bows just so, we fly east on our journey west. Because of an intangible unseen whim, a most seen and quite tangible old biplane whirs and thrashes through the sky, above a railroad track, reaching for the Atlantic Ocean.

Ahead, the sun rises from a golden sea. I need railroad tracks no longer, and shift my navigation from dull rails to a blinding star.

Sometimes there are so many symbols about me in the air that it is surprising I can see to fly. I become a symbol, myself. Which is a glorious sort of feeling, for there are so many meanings for me that I can inspect the meaning-bin and carefully select the one that looks best and feels best for this day and this hour. And all good meanings, and real.

What shall I be, this moment? For that part of me that keeps a cautious and uneasy distance from meanings, I am the holder of Commercial Airman's Certificate 1393604, with the privileges of flight instructor, rated for instrument flying and to control single- and multi-engine land airplanes through the

[23]

air and along the ground as necessary to accomplish the mission of flight. For that part of me, I am 5.27 miles from the Wilmington Omnirange, on the 263-degree radial, at 2,176 feet pressure altitude at 1118 hours Greenwich Mean Time on the 27th day of April in the 1,964th year of the Gregorian Calendar, New Style.

The fuselage of the airplane I fly is painted Stearman Vermilion, Randolph stock number 1918, the wings and tail are Champion Yellow, Randolph stock number unknown but very definitely and precisely listed somewhere in the dusty records of a forgotten drawer in a lost attic away over the horizon. A very precise airplane, every bolt and joint and stitch of it. Not only Detroit-Ryan Speedster, Model Parks P-2A, but serial number 101, registration number N499H, built December, 1929, and licensed January, 1930, under Aircraft Type Certificate 276.

Divorced from meanings, with labels only attached, the airplane and I become very complex and forbidding machines. Every bolt and wire of the engine and the airplane has a stock number, a serial number, a lot number. Take a magnifying glass, scrape away the varnish, and there are our numbers, stamped. And meaningless. When one surrounds oneself with meanings there are conflicts and shades of meanings and meanings whose holes are not drilled to line up and can't be bolted together. One can be safe, with serial numbers, in a land of utter quiet. No disputes. Nothing moves.

But I am moving now, and so would carefully select a tailored meaning to outfit my airplane and one to slip about my own shoulders.

Since it is a bright day, biplane, and promising fair, let us mean joy. How does that fit? Look: joy seeks the sun, and the early of the mornings. Joy moves with delight, hasting to where the ocean is golden and the air crisp and cold. Joy

[24]

tastes the liquid air spraying back onto leather helmet and lowered goggles. It delights in the freedom that is only found and won away up in the sky, from which there is no falling if one only keeps moving. And in the moving, we gain, and joy is precious even in Stearman Vermilion number 1918.

Here, here, son. The practical self speaking, uneasy with symbols, the rein-holding, solemn self. Here, here. All we want to do is get this thing out over the Atlantic a foot or two, so you can say you've done it, and then we have to get along on west. Engine, you know. It *could* fail.

How is it possible, I wonder, for me to be so sure, so self-centered certain that I am in control? I do not know, but the fact remains that I am, when I fly. Those clouds, for instance. Others may pass through them, but I am the one who lends them to the world. The patterns now in the sunlight on the sea, the streaks of fire in the sunrise, the cool breeze and the warm, all of these. Mine. For surely there can be in the world no one who knows and loves these as I. There, the source of the confidence and the power. I am sole heir to these, who can lift an airplane into the sky and feel, as the cloud wheels beneath him, that he has come truly home once again.

Look up, of a morning when the sun rises through the clouds, or of an evening as it sets. A thousand slanting shafts of gold, aren't there? A brilliance, a sort of molten fire hidden? These are just the sights of my land seen from the ground, so bright and so warm and with beauty filled that the cloud cannot contain it all and splashes its overflow onto the earth as just a hint of the brilliance and the gold that exists above.

That little sound of four cylinders or five or seven, above the cloud, comes from a winged machine that is immersed in bright wonder. To be up there and fly alongside this creature is to see a vision, for the wings of an airplane in the sunrise are of beaten gold, going bright silver if you catch the proper

[25]

angle, and on the canopy and along the windscreen dance the sparkle of diamonds. And within, a pilot, watching. What can you say, seeing this? You say nothing, and you share with another man in another cockpit a time of silence.

For when he sees this, when the magnificence floods over an airplane and the man who guides it, there is no speaking. Enchanted in the high land, to mention of beauty and joy in the mundane surroundings of earth and city and wall and polite society is to feel gawkish and out of place. Even to his best beloved, a pilot cannot speak of the wonder of the sky.

After the sun is high and the spell fades, one's fuel is gone. The white needle is at the E, the little indicator cork ceases its bobbing, a red low-level-warning light glares above a fuel counter. And in a minute or five or ten, the tires thud again onto the grass or scream a bluesmoke cry against the concrete of a once-forgotten runway. Mission done, flight over. Chalk up another hour. Pencil and logbook for a moment busy. But though the earth once again spreads beneath our feet, and the unnatural quiet of an engineless world surrounds us, there is new fuel to be hosed into tanks, and another page in the log to be filled.

To a pilot, the most important thing in the world is flight. To share it is the gift without price. Therein is a key to the sometimes wild acts of young pilots. They fly under bridges, they buzz housetops, they loop and roll their airplane much closer to the ground than is safe. They are a major concern of military flight-training bases, for such action reflects a lack of discipline, and occasionally means the loss of student and airplane. But his thought is to give, to share joy with those he loves, to share a truth. For pilots sometimes see behind the curtain, behind the veil of gossamer velvet, and find the truth behind man, the force behind a universe.

[26]

In the bright thread are woven four billion lives. Now and again, a man will see a certain brightness beyond the curtain and go spinning away into the depths of reality. We who remain watch him go, marvel for a moment, and return to our stations at our own crossthreads in the woof and the warp of a sparkling illusion.

For even in an airplane we see too often imperfectly. With advancing invention, with cockpits closed and navigation instruments and radio and new electronics, the problem of flying has become something to be solved more and more within an arm's distance of the pilot. Drifting off course? A needle shows it, points the error, and all the pilot must do to see it is to look within a three-inch face of glass. Concerned about weather ahead? Dial a frequency on the radio, call a meteorologist and ask expert advice. Airplane slowing in the air, approaching a stall? A red light flashes on the instrument panel, a warning horn blares. We look outside to the sky only when we have time to enjoy the view, and if we don't want to be bothered with the view, we needn't look outside from takeoff till touchdown. It is this kind of flight over which the manufacturers of flight simulators can boast, "Impossible to tell our trainer from flight itself!" And so it is. Those who define flight as a series of hours spent in attention to the moving gages of an instrument panel cannot tell the difference. The only thing that is missing is the wind. The heat of the sun. The canyons of cloud and sheer white walls rising solid at each wingtip. The sound and the sting of rain, the freezing cold of altitude, the sea of moonlight in its bed of fog, the stars untwinkling and ice-hard in a midnight sky.

So. The biplane. Is it the better way? If the Parks flies too slowly, there are no warning horns or flashing red lights. Just a shudder in the control stick and it turns into a machine unwilling to be controlled, suddenly aware that it is heavier than the air. One must be careful and alert for the shudder. One must look outside, for outside is flight itself, the moving through the air and knowing it. Especially, knowing it.

Navigation is goggles down, look over the side, down through the churning winds. The railroad: so. The river crossing: so. But the lake, there should be a lake here. Perhaps there are headwinds. . . .

A check on the weather is a constant thing. The clouds mass and grow together, lowering into the hills. Slanting columns of rain, where earlier there was no rain. What to do, pilot, what to do? Beyond the hills, the cloud may thin, or break. But then, beyond the hills, the cloud can lower to brush the grasstops ragged and soak them in rain. Hills are green coffins for the airplanes and pilots who judge wrongly. Beware the hills when the cool grey mist is pulled over your eyes.

Decide, pilot. Land now? Choose the pasture for soft touchdown and certainty of longer living? Or push on, into the grey? This is flight: decisions. And knowing that sooner or later an airplane must always come to rest.

We turn south, the Parks and I, to follow the Atlantic coastline. The beach is wide and hard and deserted, and the only sounds across it are the sounds of the wind and the waves crashing and the cry of a seagull and the brief windy passing roar of an airplane flying. The air is salt air, and salt spray leaps toward the tall wheels of the biplane. Here for a hundred miles we can fly in comfort with the wheels skimming the wave tops, for the old fliers' caution—always be able to land safely should the engine stop—is satisfied by the wide

[28]

smooth expanse of sand to our right. There is no greater security for a pilot than the security of flat land nearby. Flat land equals peace of mind and serenity in any situation. Fail the engine, bring the downdraft, bring the storms with thunder rolling; with a level field nearby, the pilot has no worry. A circle once to lose altitude, a gentle lifting of the nose, and airplane and pilot are blessed with their only time without the pressure and the need for constant motion. To fly above flat fields is to fly without pressure, and is the most relaxed flying that a pilot can know. And now from horizon to horizon as far as I can see ahead is the broad flat landing beach of South Carolina.

But, oddly enough, the biplane does not feel right, as if she is not glad to be here. There is foreboding in her, a sense of caution that dampens even the assurance of the infinite beach strip ahead. What could be wrong? Why, I simply am not used to her yet, or she to me. It will take time, it will take a few hours to fly this beach and enjoy it to its full.

A brief inlet, with a single small sailboat drifting idly along. We roar over its mast, with one quick wave to the skipper at the helm, and catch his wave in return.

The shape of the land now, and of the beach, is familiar. I know that to the right there should be a swamp soon, and soon to the right there is a swamp. How can I know? A map can give no such familiarity, for ink and colored lines, unless studied and imagined, are only ink and colored lines. And this is familiar, the curve of the beach, the swamp.

Of course! I have been here before! I have flown this very stretch of beach; and the vagueness and the familiarity come from a different viewpoint. I have flown the beach before at an altitude many times higher than the biplane will ever reach, from eight miles in the air, and looked down upon these same sands and have noted with satisfaction that my ground-speed was six hundred miles per hour. A different day then, and a different airplane. Fine days, those. Of strapping into thirteen-ton fighters and riding the twisting thundering heat of a turbine engine. Climb straight up, come blasting straight down through the speed of sound.

A good life, and it was sad to leave the fighters with their great speed and their brilliant glory. But I nodded my head to circumstance and the reins were snapped and the days of machmeters and gunsights faded behind me.

Yet the high land is the same no matter the vehicle. With a whirling thrashing propeller again in front of the cockpit instead of a spinning turbine behind, I discover that the only real difference is that a tank of fuel lasts three times as long, and in place of speed I am the master of time, and a new kind of freedom.

Suddenly, on the beach below a sunrise biplane in the world of now, a house. Two houses. Five, and a wooden pier stretching out into the sea. A water tower, and the name,

CRESCENT BEACH. We have arrived. Time for fuel and a sandwich.

Still, though, the foreboding, the reluctance in the wood and the fabric and a trembling in the control stick.

The airport is a single runway, a hard-surface runway not far from the water tower. The wind is blowing from the sea, across the runway. Official terminology: crosswind. I have heard the stories of the old pilots. Never land in a crosswind, they said, and told stories of the days when to do this was a painful and costly error.

And for a moment I forget what time it is. The airport is safe in 1964 and I am flying in 1929.

Come on, airplane, settle down. The Parks feels brittle and stiff, and I move the rudder from side to side to make her loosen up. She is trying to remind me of the stories. Crosswinds to her are like flames to a racehorse, and I am leading her, urging her into the heat and the fire, concerned only about fuel and sandwiches.

Eighty miles per hour and lined on the runway. Power back, the Parks settles lifelessly toward the ground. I am puzzled that she should feel so dead. Settle down, there, little friend. In a minute you will be drinking a tank of cool red eighty-octane.

The wheels touch the concrete smoothly at 70 mph, and, tail held high, we slow, runway blurred still at the edges. Finally the tail loses its flying speed and the tailwheel comes down to squeak on the hard surface. And we meet the inevitable. Moving at thirty miles per hour, the biplane, against her will and mine, begins to turn into the wind. Sudden full rudder against the turn has no effect, and she swings faster into the wind. Press hard opposite brake . . . but that instant when the brake could have helped is past and from the slow turn a monster grabs the biplane and slams her

[31]

into an instant whiplash turnabout. With a great shriek from the tires we snap around, sliding sideways down the runway. A shriek, a horizon blurring all around, a sharp pistol-shot from the right main landing gear, all in a half-second. While I sit powerless in the cockpit, numbly holding full opposite rudder, a wheel breaks, folds beneath the airplane. A wingtip grinds suddenly down into the concrete, spraying sparks and splinters and old fabric to mix with blue burning rubber smoke. Scraping and screaming about me, the biplane is lashed once, hard, by her old enemy, the crosswind.

And then it is quiet, save for the engine panting and quickly dying as I cut the switches.

You fool.

You stupid idiot you harebrained excuse for a pilot you hamfisted imbecile. You idiot you fool you dumb stupid—you've broken her! Look at what you've done, you idiot, you fool! I climb slowly from the cockpit. It has been very quick, very sudden, and I have destroyed an airplane because I didn't heed the old warnings. Nineteen twenty-nine does not mix with today. They are separate separate worlds. You fool. The right wheel is smashed beneath the airplane and torn in two pieces. You idiot. The right wingtip is shredded, the rear wingspar cracked. You dumb stupid imbecile. I forced 1929 into the present and that force was enough to shear the carbon-steel bolts of the right main gear fittings, to twist them into little bent-clay cylinders of something once useful. You worthless clod.

A few tears of gasoline fall from the engine. It is very quiet on the runway. The crosswind sighs now, unconcerned, no longer interested.

Airport attendants, those that heard the crash, drive from the hangar with a truck and a winch and they lift the nose of the biplane, and help me guide her under a roof. A tall jack is

[32]

moved in to replace the missing wheel and broken landing gear strut.

They leave me and I sit alone with the biplane. What is the lesson, airplane? What am I supposed to learn here? There is no answer. Outside, the sky goes dark, and later it begins to rain.

# 4

"Is that all that's wrong?" Colonel George Carr speaking, and the words echo in the hangar. "From the way Evander talked, I thought you had HURT something! Son of a gun, boy, we'll have you flying by tomorrow noon!"

George Carr. A collection of letters that stands for a weatherbeaten face below a shock of grey hair and warm blue eyes that have seen many calendars come and go, and many, many airplanes.

The call to Lumberton, this morning, had not been easy to make.

"Evander, I'm at Crescent Beach."

"You're fine, I hope," Evander Britt said. "And how's your new airplane flying? Still like it?"

I was grateful for the straight-line. "I like it fine, Van. But I don't think it's too crazy about me."

[34]

"Now how would you mean that?" If he thought from my call that something had gone wrong, he was certain of it now.

"I had a bit of a ground-loop here, trying to land in a crosswind. Lost a gear and a wheel, tore one wing up pretty bad. Wonder if you'd happen to have a spare gear and wheel around." There. I had said it. Whatever he says now I deserve. The worst thing he can say, I deserve every bit of it. I clenched my teeth.

"Oh . . . no . . ."

For a moment there was full silence on the line, when he knew that he had given his airplane to the wrong man, to a brash cocky youngster who hadn't begun to learn how to fly an airplane or to be a pilot. The silence was not enjoyable.

"Well." He was brisk and friendly again, all business, trying to solve my problems. "I've got a spare set of landing gear all right, that you can have. And a set of wings, if you need. You broke the wheel, did you?"

"Right main wheel. Tire looks usable, but there's not a chance for the wheel."

"I don't have any wheels. Maybe Gordon Sherman, over in Asheville, might loan you one to get home on. I'll call him up now and drive over and get it if he does. . . . Don't know what we're going to do if he doesn't have one. Those big wheels scarcer than hens' teeth. I'll call George Carr the minute I hang up. He's done all the mechanic work on the Parks, and licensed it for you. If anyone can fix the Parks, he can. I'll put the landing gear and wheel in his car, if he'll drive down. I'd be down myself, but I've got a case going in court tomorrow that I just can't leave. You have the airplane in a hangar, do you?"

"Yes."

"That's good. We're having some rain up here, moving down that way. Wouldn't want to get her wet." He paused.

[35]

"If you want to have your Fairchild back, I'm making the offer."

"Thanks, Van. I got my airplane right now. All I have to do is learn how to fly it."

George Carr had arrived, windshield wipers squeaking across battered glass, three hours later.

"Why don't you strip the fabric off around that aileron fitting there, so we can get at it a little easier? Might pull that panel beneath the wing, too, would help."

The colonel works happily, because he likes to work on airplanes. He likes to see them come back to life beneath his hands. He is pounding with a rawhide mallet on a twisted bracket, straightening it. Pound, pound, echoing.

". . . used to take my old Kreider-Reisner 31 out Sundays, land on the crossroads. People for the most part never seen an airplane up close before, let alone got in one." Pound. Pound pound-pound. "Yeah. For a while there it was a pretty good livin'." Pound-pound-pound.

He talks on, as we work, of a world that I am just beginning to know. A world in which a pilot always has to be ready to repair his airplane, or it will never fly again. He speaks without nostalgia or longing for the days past, as though they weren't really past at all, as though as soon as he has the wheel back on the biplane we'll start the engine and fly to a crossroad or a pasture close to town, to begin flying the folk who have never seen an airplane up close before, let alone got in one.

"Looks like that ought to do the job." The pounded aileron fitting is straight and flat as a concrete hangar floor. "Stronger than it was before. Cold-worked, you know."

Perhaps I haven't been born too late, after all. Perhaps it isn't too late to learn. I have been brought up in a world of airplanes with the white stars of the military upon their wings, and U.S. AIR FORCE stenciled beneath gunports. Of airplanes repaired by specialists, in accordance with T.O.1–F84F–2, of flying procedures prescribed by Air Force Regulation 60–16, of conduct controlled by the Universal Code of Military Justice. There is, in all of this, no regulation that allows a pilot to repair his own airplane, for that requires a special army of technicians with a special army of serial numbers and job classifications. Airplanes and parts of airplanes in the military service are rarely repaired at all—they are replaced. Radio fading and going dim in flight? Corrective action: remove and replace. Engine operated overtemperature? Remove and replace. Landing gear strut collapse after touchdown? Class 26: aircraft removed from service.

And here is George Carr, barnstormer, mechanic, with a rawhide mallet in his hand, saying it would all be stronger than ever. I learn that the repairing or rebuilding of an airplane, or of a man, doesn't depend upon the condition of the original. It depends upon the attitude with which the job is taken. The magic phrase, "Is THAT all that's wrong!" and an attitude to match, and the real job of rebuilding is finished.

"Gordon Sherman's loaning you a wheel from his Eaglerock to get home on; 'Vander Britt put it out in the trunk of the car." He is straining now over a heavy bolt on the landing gear leg. "You might run . . . the wheel . . . down to the gas station . . . and see if they can put the tire on for us."

As simple as that. Gordon Sherman is loaning you a wheel. A rare old 30-by-5 spun-aluminum wheel, the kind that aren't built now and haven't been built for thirty years and that never will be built again. On loan from a friend I never met. Perhaps Gordon Sherman had wondered how he'd feel a continent away from home, in need of a rare old wheel for his Eaglerock. Perhaps he has wheels to spare. Perhaps his basement is filled with 30-by-5 spun aluminum wheels. But Gordon Sherman is this moment silently thanked by a friend he has never met, and will be thanked, silently, for a long time after.

Colonel George Carr works on into the night, under the green fluorescent lights of the hangar at Crescent Beach, South Carolina. He works and he directs and I learn from him until 1:30 A.M. At 1:30 A.M. the biplane is patched, and ready to fly.

"You might fly her over toward North Carolina tomorrow," he says, grinning, not knowing that at 1:30 in the morning people are supposed to be dead tired and ready to drop instantly asleep, "and we'll put the finishing touches on her there. There's some fabric around the shop, and some dope. We'll put you to work doping."

And it is done. He lifts his clanking, boulder-heavy tool kit into the car, sets the torn wheel carefully beside it, and with a wave disappears into the darkness, driving back to Lumberton. Exit, for the moment, a teacher of confidence. Exit a window into what, until one knows better, one calls the past. By the time he is home, I am asleep on the hangar floor, having spent half an hour listening to the rain, thinking that there are only twenty-six hundred miles to go.

In the morning, one patched biplane, yellow fabric held together here and there with bright red tape, lifts away from Crescent Beach, following from above a river, a highway, a railroad track, and arrives again at Lumberton, North Carolina.

Turn into the wind, touch the grass, taxi to the hangar where the colonel waits, readying fabric and dope.

Evander Britt is inspecting the taped wing before the propeller has stopped turning, running his hand lightly over the tape, feeling for broken ribs.

[38]

"You got a broken rib out here, Dick."

"I know."

"And I see you welded a plate onto the main landing gear fitting. Cracked out down there, was it?"

"Little crack, where it started to give before the bolt sheared. Welded the plate on, and it shouldn't want to crack any more." As long as we are talking, the guilt on my shoulders doesn't hurt. It hurts when Evander Britt is silent, and looks at the biplane.

"If you want to trade back for your Fairchild . . ."

"Evander, I want this airplane and I know I don't deserve it. I'm going to fly it home if it takes me all year, if I have to pick it up in a box and carry it to California." That is probably the wrong thing to say. After this start, the chances of my having to pick up the pieces and carry them west are much greater than the chances of the biplane flying there under her own power. There is little doubt that the lawyer would like to have his airplane safely again in his hangar instead of chasing around the country with a novice pilot in its cockpit. There is less than little doubt. There is no doubt at all.

"Well, if you ever want to . . ." he says, looking again at the taped wing. "Boy, you sounded miserable as a wet rooster on that telephone. Like a little old soaking-wet banty rooster. Like the whole world had just come down on your head."

"Sure wasn't very happy. That was a stupid thing, trying to land in that wind. It was really stupid."

"Well, don't feel bad about it, boy. These things happen. Come on now. Roll up your sleeves and we'll help George get her fixed better than new."

I learn about repairing wood-and-cloth airplanes. The colonel shows me how to cut a patch of Grade A cotton fabric and fray the edges, and smooth it to the wing with clear dope, let it dry and sand it smooth. Another coat of clear dope,

[39]

another sanding. Then colored dope and sanding, over and over, until I can't tell the patch from the rest of the fabric around. After many patches, at last finished and better than new, it is afternoon and time to turn the nose westward, and fly.

"What do I owe you, George?" This is a hard time, when the business has to come to the front and the learning and the friendship of working together on an airplane take a back seat.

"Oh, I don't know. Didn't really do much. You did most of the work." He rummages in a tool bin, looking for his pipe tobacco.

"The devil I did. Wasn't for you, this airplane would be sitting in that hangar at Crescent Beach till the junkman came to haul her away. What do I owe you?"

A week ago, in Wichita, the tailwheel on the Fairchild had been replaced. A four-hour job, by businesslike modern-day mechanics. Cost: $90.75, parts and labor and tax included. What should it cost, then, to replace aileron fittings that had been smashed flat and immovable, install new shock cord on a main gear leg, install a new wheel, repair a wingtip and ribs and spar and cover the whole with fabric; parts, labor and tax included?

George Carr is awkward and uncomfortable and for a full twenty minutes I point out that my thanks aren't going to buy him dinner tonight or replace the dope and fabric I have used, or buy back the sleep that he missed or even the gasoline that he used driving to Crescent Beach.

"Name a figure, then," he says. "Whatever you say will be fine with me."

"Five hundred dollars is what it would cost me, assuming I could have found somebody that even knew where a spar is in a biplane."

"Don't be silly."

"I'm not being silly. When was the last time you had to pay the going rates to have some work done on an airplane, George? You're the world's best mechanic, sir, but the world's worst businessman. Come on, now. I have to get going before the sun's down. I can't leave till I pay you something. I won't be able to look at myself in the morning if I walk out of here without paying you. Honest. And I really am sorry."

A small shy voice from across the room. "Thirty, forty dollars be too much?"

I argue for a while and work him up to strike an agreement at fifty dollars, which leaves me just enough money to finish the trip across the country, but still feeling like a young and heartless overlord taking advantage of the kind and gentle people who dwell about him. And I feel at the same time, helplessly, that I am committing a sacrilege. For George Carr and I love the same machines and the same joys. I can't help but believe that in the short time we spent working together over the biplane we each earned a friend. What kind of person is it who offers blind money to a friend in return for an act of friendship?

But the others, who were not my friends, those sheer brisk businessmen repairing a tailwheel, had handsomely charged and been handsomely paid. It isn't fair.

The biplane takes her throttle well, and lifts quickly into the wind. A last wing-rocking pass over the hangar and over two tiny figures on the grass, waving, and we point our nose again into the sun, swinging swiftly down out of its high arc toward certain collision with an immovable horizon.

How many collisions, sun? How many times have you dropped from high focused white heat down through the

[41]

same cooling arc and fallen into the same valley that you will fall into this evening? And across the world, every moment a sunrise, and a new day beginning.

The sun moves another tenth of a degree toward the horizon, and as I fly, the valley that would have received it becomes a little lake, all golden, a mirror of a golden sky. And then a forest of trees moves in to stand pretender to the final resting place of the sun. If I could stand still in the air, I would be able to believe that the sun truly sinks into that valley, that lake, that forest. But the biplane dispels old illusions as quickly and as firmly as she creates new ones.

One that she is working on now: the engine will run forever. Listen: 1–3–5–2–4, over and again and again and again. If there is no faltering now, there will never be a faltering. I am strong and powerful and I shall spin my bright propeller until the sun itself is weary of rising and of setting.

The ground now is going dark, and the surface of the land is one smooth pool of shadow. Once again the biplane reminds me that she has no lights for flying or landing. Even the flashlight is out of reach, in the front cockpit.

Fine thing this could be. Spend your time daydreaming and wake to find yourself enveloped in night. Find a place to land, son, or there will be more repairs for you to make. At 1740 revolutions per minute, fifty-two gallons of gasoline will last five hours and six minutes. Which means, at the moment, that there are three hours and twenty-one minutes left for my brave engine. My five-cylindered companion and its faithful flashing blade will cease to turn at just the moment that the sun sets in San Francisco, and that it rises in Jakarta. Then, perhaps, twenty-five minutes of silent gliding and the end of

the world. For the sky is the only world, quite literally the only world there is for an airplane and for the man who flies it. The other world with its flowers and its seas and its mountains and deserts is a doorway to dying for the craft and the man of the sky, unless they return very gently, very carefully, seeing where they touch.

It is time to land now, while I still can see. And let us see. Over the side, down through the deep wind, we have a few darkening pastures, a puzzlework forest of black pines, a little town. And look at that, an airport. Beacon going green . . . going white . . . going green . . . and a short double row of white pinpoints in the dark; runway lights. Come along, airplane, let us go down and sleep against the earth tonight.

Tomorrow will be a big day.

## 5

MORNING, SUN ONCE AGAIN, and a fresh green wind stirring across the wing that shelters me. A cool wind, and so fresh out of the forest that it is pure oxygen blowing. But warm in the sleeping bag and time for another moment of sleep. And I sleep to dream of the first morning that I ever flew in an airplane. . . .

Morning, sun, and a fresh green wind. Softly softly it moves, hushing gently, curving smoothly, easily, about the light-metal body of a little airplane that waits still and quiet on the emerald grass.

I will learn, in time, of relative wind, of the boundary layer and of the thermal thicket at Mach Three. But now I do not know, and the wind is wind only, soft and cool. I wait by the airplane. I wait for a friend to come and teach me to fly.

The distant seashell hush of a small-town morning is in the

air, whispering along with the early wind. You have missed much, city dweller, the words trace in smoky thought. Sleep in your concrete shell until the sun is high and forfeit the dawn. Forfeit cool wind and quiet seashell roar, forfeit carpet of tall wet grass and soft silence of the early wind. Forfeit cold airplane waiting and the footstepsound of a man who can teach you to fly.

"Morning."

"Hi."

"Get that tiedown over there, will you?" He doesn't have to speak loudly to be heard. The morning wind is no opponent for the voice of a man.

The tiedown rope is damp and prickly, and when I pull it through the lift strut's metal ring, the sound of it whirs and echoes in the morning. Symbolic, this. Loosing an airplane from the ground.

"We'll just take it easy this morning. You can relax and get the feel of the airplane; straight and level, a few turns, look over the area a bit. . . ."

We are settled in the cockpit, and I learn how to fasten the safety belt over my lap. A bewildering array of dials on the dashboard; the quiet world is shut away outside a metal-doored cabin fitted to a metal-winged, rubber-tired entity with words cast into the design of the rudder pedals. Luscombe, the words say. They are wellworn words and impartial, but flair and excitement were cast into the mold. Luscombe. A kind of airplane. Taste that strange exciting word. Luscombe.

The man beside me has been making little motions among the switches on the bewildering panel. He does not seem to be confused.

"Clear."

[46]

I have no idea what he means. Clear. Why should he say clear?

A knob is pulled, one knob chosen at this moment from many samelooking knobs. And there goes my quiet dawn.

The harsh rasp of metal against metal and gear against gear, the labored grind of a small electric motor turning a great mass of enginemetal and propeller steel. Not the sound of an automobile engine starter. A starter for the engine of an airplane. Then, as if a hidden switch was pressed, the engine is running, shattering stillness with multibursts of gasoline and fire. How can he think in all this noise? How can he know what to do next? The propeller has been a blur for seconds, a disc that shimmers in the early sun. A mystic, flashing disc, rippling early light and bidding us follow. It leads us, rubber wheels rolling, along a wide grass road, in front of other airplanes parked and tied, dead and quiet. The road leads to the end of a wide level fairway.

He holds the brakes and pushes a lever that makes the noise unbearable. Is there something wrong with the airplane? Is this flying? We are strapped into our seats, compressed into this little cabin, assailed by a hundred decibels running. Perhaps I would rather not fly. Luscombe is a strange word and it means small airplane. Small and loud and built of metal. Is this the dream of flight?

The sound dies away for a moment. He leans toward me, and I toward him, to hear his words.

"Looks good. You ready?"

I nod. I am ready. We might as well get it over with. He had said it would be fun, and had said the words with the strange soft tone he used, belying his smile, when he truly meant his words. For that meaning I had come, had left a comfortable bed at five in the morning to tramp through wet

[47]

grass and cold wind. Let's get it over with and trouble me no more with your flying.

The lever is again forward, the noise again unbearable, but this time the brakes are loosed, and the little airplane, the Luscombe, surges ahead. It carries us along, down the fairway.

Into the sky.

It really happened. We were rolling, following the magic spinning brightflashing blade, and suddenly we were rolling no more.

A million planes I had seen flying. A million planes, and was unimpressed. Now it was I, and that green dwindling beneath the wheels, that was the ground. Separating me from the green grass and quiet ground? Air. Thin, unseen, blowable, breathable air. Air is nothing. And between us and the ground: a thousand feet of nothing.

The noise? A little hum.

There! The sun! Housetops aglint, and chimney smoke rising!

The metal? Wonderful metal.

Look! The horizon! I can see beyond the horizon! I can see to the end of the world!

We fly! By God, *we fly!*

My friend watches me and he is smiling.

The wind stirs the flap of my sleeping bag and the sun is already above the horizon. It is 6:15 and time to get up and get moving. The wind is not just cool; the wind is cold. Cold! And I thought spring in the South was a languid time of liquid warm from dawn to dawn. Into the chilled flight suit and pull on the frozen boots and the icy leather jacket. The airport is flat and closed about me and the runway lights are still on. Breakfast at the next stop, then, and time now to get

the engine started and warming. One must always let the old engines warm themselves well before flight. They need ten minutes running on the ground to get the cold out of their oil and life into their controls.

Despite the cold, engine start is a beautiful time of day. The routine: pull the propeller through five times, fuel valve on, mixture rich, seven shots of priming fuel, pull the prop through two more times, magneto switch on, pump the throttle, crank the inertia starter, run back to the cockpit, engage the starter and swallow exhaust and engine thunder unfiltered and loud and frozen sharp, shattering again the silence of a little airport.

How many times have I started an airplane engine, even in the few years that I have been flying? In how many airplanes? So many different ways, so many different sounds, but beneath them all the same river; they are symbols of one meaning.

"Clear!"

Pull the starter knob to send the propeller into a faltering blurred arc. Press the primer knob. And from the exhaust stacks a cloud of blue and a storm of sound. Inspect the cloud under a microscope and you would find tiny drops of oil unburned. Inspect the sound on an oscilloscope and trace a quickchanging world of harsh pointed lines under the reference grid. In neither instrument can the essence of engine start be caught. That essence is unseen, in the thought of the one who controls the bank of switches that bid an engine to life. Get the prop turning, check the oil pressure, let the engine warm up. About 900 rpm for a minute or two. Forward on the throttle until the wheels begin to roll. Taxi to the waiting runway.

How many times in the history of flight has the routine been followed? From the earliest days, when engine start was the signal for ground crew to throw themselves on the stabilizer, holding a brakeless airplane until the wave of the pilot's hand. Through the days in the sun of war when engine start was the crashing roaring climax to "Run One . . . mesh One . . ." and the steepfalling whine of the inertia starter. To the days when now and then along the line of the crew's checklist there is the softest of purring rumbles, and the only visible sign of an engine alive is the quick-rising needle of the tailpipe temperature gage, and the first ripples of heat drifting back from smooth-cowled turbines.

But for every one, for every single one, engine start is journey start. If you would seek some of the romance of flight, watch when the engines first begin to turn. Pick any place in aviation history, in any kind of airplane, and there is a shard or a massive block of romance, of glory and glamour. The pilot, in the cockpit, readies himself and his airplane. In scores of languages, in a hundred different terms, there comes the moment when one word or one sign means: Go.

"CLEAR!"

"CONTACT!"

". . . mesh One."

". . . OK. Start One."

"Clear left."

"Lightoff."

A green flare in the sky.

A flight leader's finger, drawing a quick circle in the air.

"PILOTS. START YOUR ENGINES."

"Hit it."

"Let's go."

Great black massive propellers slam suddenly around. External power carts stagger and nearly die under instant load of high amperage. The explosion of shotgun starters. Hiss and ground-shaking concussion of compressed-air starters. Rattle

[51]

and clatter and labored moan of hand-cranked inertia fly-wheels. The snap and clack of impulse magnetos. Roar of external air to the air-driven turbine starters. Slow soft acceleration of squaretipped turboprop blades.

From stillness into motion. From death into life. From silence into rising thunder. And each a part of the journey, for every man in every cockpit.

There is sound and glory, blue smoke and thunder, for anyone who wishes. Descendants of pioneers need not mourn the passing of an untouched frontier; it waits quiet above their heads. Little difference makes the look of the machine that becomes soon a part of the pioneer. He can be on flight orders, with a military commission signed by the president of the nation, riding forty thousand pounds of thrust at twice the speed of sound, protected by inch-thick glass and an artificial atmosphere within his cockpit. Despite the restrictions of the military, he has still his taste of freedom, his sight of the sky. Or he can be on the orders of desire and conscience alone, with an airplane bought instead of a second automobile, traveling a hundred miles per hour and protected from the wind by an eighth inch of plexiglass or by a leather helmet and a pair of goggles.

The journey has been traveled tens of thousands of times, a trail blazed by Montgolfier and Montgomery and Wright, hewn and cleared by Lincoln Beachy and Glenn Curtiss and Earle Ovington and Jack Knight, paved and smoothed and widened by every man that guided an airplane away from the earth or who spent an hour in the dream of flight. Yet, in the billions of hours that men have been aloft, not one has left a mark in the sky. Into the smooth sky we pull a tiny wake of rippled air. When our airplane is gone, the sky smooths, carefully covering every sign of our passing, and becomes the quiet wilderness that it has always been.

So call the *clear!* and starter engaged. Breathe blue smoke and set the wheels to rolling. Oil pressure and temperature and valve the fuel and set the flaps for takeoff. Set propeller revolutions to tremble at the redline, submerge in a sea of sound and bright glory. And go the way along the path, take up the journey in solitude.

Today our task is to cross the land in giant steps, to move as far as we can westward before the sun again wins its race.

A quick engine runup, feeling again the goodness of being a long way from home and having an engine check out precisely as it should.

Throttle forward, a cloud of early dust, and we are airborne once again. Splashing green fountains of spring trees roll below as we settle into cruising flight, to share the joy of other machines and other people who are only happy when they are moving.

The hand on the control stick, testing elevators and rudder, the fingers on the magneto switch, the voice, *"Contact!,"* each a part of one who seeks horizons lost a thousand years ago. "This time," the thought. "Maybe this time." The search, always the search. On a routine trip, over lands crossed daily on Flight 388, from the crowded flight deck of a jet airliner and from the cockpit of a sport airplane, the eyes of the wanderer look down, seeking the hidden; Elysium overlooked, the happy valley undiscovered. Now and again, the wanderer stiffens quickly in his cockpit, points down for the co-pilot to see, banks a wing for a clearer view. But the grass is never quite green enough; those are weeds at the water's edge, a strip of barren ground between the meadow and the river. Every once in a while the ideal is mirrored in the sky. Every once in a while there is a moment's perfection: the cloud, hard and brilliant against a hard and brilliant sky.

Wind and cloud and sky; common denominators in perfection, eternals. The ground you can change. Rip out the grass, level the hill, pour a city over it all. But rip out the wind? Bury a cloud in concrete? Twist the sky to the image in one man's mind? Never.

We search for one goal and find another. We search the visible, holding the polished memory of perfection that was, and in the tens and hundreds and thousands of hours that we drift through the sky we discover a much different perfection. We journey toward a land of joy, and in our search we find the way that other, earlier pilots have scouted before us. They spoke of solitude in the high places, and we find the solitude. They spoke of storms; the storms are there, glowering still. They spoke of high sun and dark skies and stars clearer than ground ever saw; all of them remain.

If I could talk now to a barnstormer or read his words on the yellowed pages of 1929, he would tell me of flying the south, on the route from Columbia, South Carolina, to Augusta, Georgia. It's the easiest thing in the world to follow a railroad, but out of Columbia there's such a twist and tangle of railroad it takes a good eye to sort the tracks that lead to Augusta from the ones that lead to Chattahoochee, to Mirabel, to Oak Hollow. Follow the wrong one, he would say, and you find yourself off in the middle of nowhere, and not much of an idea how to get back.

And it's true. *Look* at the mass of railroads down there! Maybe there's an air molecule or two around that remembers the flash of his propeller, that might chuckle at my concern, coming along so much later, over precisely the same problem that caused his concern before me. We both must find our way out of the maze, and find it by ourselves. I don't know what he did, but I look ahead to pick the sharp arrowhead of a lake on course, and fly to that and pick the railroad then,

[54]

when there is clearly only one choice to make. Perhaps he had a better way. I wish he were around still; I wish that I could look out and see his Jenny or his J-1 Standard smoothing along above the twin rails. But this morning I continue alone, or at least as far as my eyes can see, alone. The history and the tradition and the old molecules are here about me every second. The barnstorming pilots said that the sky was cold and that they froze in their cockpits. I know now that they kept warm for some time by simply not believing that it could possibly be so cold over the south, where, after all, people come to flee the ice of northern winters. But at last there is no fighting left to be done; the lesson is learned. It gets terribly cold; hard, ice-freezing cold over South Carolina in the morning of a spring day. I used to smile when I heard of the early pilots huddling forward under what little shelter they could get from the windscreen, and shuffling their feet quickly back and forth in odd strange movements just for the sake of moving and keeping the cold at bay.

I am not smiling now. Instead I discover a technique on my own, over South Carolina. I won't be so brash as to think that it hasn't been discovered scores of times before, in the same air, in fact, by scores of early pilots. There is a huge imaginary crank on a shaft thrust through the center of the instrument panel. Turn it. Turn it faster and faster with the right glove, reverse it and turn it faster still with the left glove. If you turn that crank long enough and fast enough, it just barely keeps you from going numb and blue in the cold. And it makes you so tired you can hardly muster strength to look over the icy side and down to check where the winds are drifting you now.

The sun in South Carolina is timed to begin to warm the air precisely one second before the frost-covered pilot decides to call a halt to all this nonsense and land and start a gasoline fire

[55]

to warm himself. Fleece-lined leather jacket, woolen flight suits and shirts and rabbit-fur gloves don't make a bit of difference. The only thing that steps in at that last second is the sun, throwing a billion BTU's into the earth, and gradually, very gradually, beginning to warm the air. Old pilots, wherever you are now, I can report that the mornings of the South Carolina spring are exactly as you left them.

Always they looked for places to land should the engine suddenly stop, and always do I. That is one of the old habits that has disappeared. The odds against a modern engine failing during any one flight are astronomical. The odds against it failing during any one moment of any one flight, while the pilot happens to be considering a place to land, is out of the realm of ordinary mathematics. So, beyond a bit of lip service, forced landings in modern airplanes are no longer practiced. Why bother, if an engine will never fail? Spins and spin recoveries have not been taught for years. We have horns and lights that warn against the conditions under which an unknowing pilot can manhandle an airplane into a spin. And if an airplane will never be spun, why bother to teach spin recoveries? Why bother to teach aerobatics? The chance that a pilot could save his life by knowing how to control an airplane when it is in a vertical bank or when it has been tossed upside down are rather remote, because unless one flies into extreme turbulence or crosses the wake of a jet transport, the chances are remote that the airplane will ever know more than a shallow bank. Besides, most modern airplanes are not licensed for aerobatics.

Gone the old skills. Don't listen to the wind to tell your airspeed, watch the airspeed indicator and hope that it is correct. Don't look over the side to gage your altitude, trust the altimeter, and don't forget to set it properly before each flight. Make the proper numbers appear in the proper dials at

[56]

the proper time, and you have a first-class automobile with wings.

But no need for bitterness, for when I say gone the old skills, I don't speak true. The old skills and the old days are there for those who would seek them out.

One hour, the end of the railroad track, and the town of Augusta. Lower into the warming air, and left-rudder-left-stick in a wide sweeping turn about the airport. There the windsock, saying the winds are almost calm this morning. There a pattern of runways, which I disregard, and rows of grass between, to which I pay very close attention. There the red fuel pumps, with no customer so early in the morning.

No customers in the sky this morning, either. I am alone. A little more aileron, to bank the wings up vertically and drop quickly toward the grass. Grass isn't often landed upon at airports, and one must be careful to look at it closely for traces of rabbit holes hidden and gullies crossing. The biplane skims the grasstops and there is not far down to look to see the ground. It looks good for landing.

Forward on the throttle for a burst of power, a long climbing turn to the left, in a pattern that will bring us lined once again on the grass, this time to land.

In three minutes I fly the last turn to line up with the grass and have one last chance to look at it. Then, look out, rabbits. All there is ahead is a wide expanse of cherry-lemon fabric, braces and crossbraces humming, a shining aluminum cowl, an oil-sprayed front windscreen, black engine cylinders, the blur of a propeller idling around, here and there a little triangle of sky peeking, to the sides a slow blur of grass flowing, and sudden hard hard rolling of the wheels on the cold ground and the brittle cold grassblades by the thousands splintering underwheel and this is the time we really go to work on the

[57]

rudder pedals to keep it straight keep it straight and right about here is where we lost it in the crosswind and remember the way she just started to go around and there was nothing you could do about it left-rudder-right-rudder-left but we just about got this one wired and my gosh it sure didn't take us long to get stopped and it's a nice feeling to be under control again and able to S-turn and see ahead and move slowly along.

An easy turn around, grassblades splintering now only by the scores and if I wanted I could get out right here and walk on the grass. The biplane is no longer an airplane, but a big awkward three-wheeled teetery vehicle pulled along by the most inefficient expedient of a fan turning around on its nose.

We roll onto the concrete of a taxiway and the bumps and rills of the grass are gone. From traveling through the air of 1929, I have moved, through the process called "landing," back into the world of new concrete taxiways and will the gasoline, sir, be cash or credit?

Sometimes, when you taxi back into Modern, they're a bit too quick on the service. It takes a minute to get the roar out of your ears and you should be allowed a moment to take off your helmet and enjoy taking it off, and feel the calm and enjoy it, and unstrap the seat belt and the parachute harness knowing that any time you can get out and walk around and have a root beer or stand and warm at a heater in the flight office. You can't envy the pilots who fly the modern sky. You have to feel sorry for them, if they haven't tucked somewhere away the joy of taking off a brown leather helmet and unstrapping from an old airplane hot-engined after its return to the earth.

Bright sun. Cold, still; but bright. I am for a moment tempted to seek the warmth of the flight office, and its maps, and its telephone to the great web of information about winds

[58]

and weather across the country this morning. But aside, temptation, and away, evil thought. One never leaves the needs of an antique for another to fill. A creed among those who fly old airplanes? In part. But more binding, the fact that the pilot is the only one who knows how to service his machine. A simple little thing, to fill a gasoline tank. But one day one pilot was forced to land in a pasture with his propeller standing still and straight in front of him, the pistons of the engine frozen in their cylinders. The one time that he was too cold, and passed the servicing of his old airplane to another, his oil tank was filled with gasoline, for the two tank caps were similar and close together. A stupid mistake, almost an inconceivable one, but the knowledge that it was stupid and that it was inconceivable offered little comfort to him when the propeller ceased to turn.

The truest reason that I stand this day cold, crouching between the wings, threaded through the jungle of struts and wires and holding the black python of a fuel hose to the tank, is not that I obey a creed or fear another's error. I stand here because I must learn to know my airplane and give her a chance to know me. In flight, hour on hour, it is the airplane that does the work; engine absorbing many thousand detonations each minute, and heats and pressures that I couldn't absorb for a second. The wires and the struts and the fabric on the wings are holding in the air twenty-three hundred pounds of airplane and fuel and pilot and equipment and doing it in a hundred-mile-per-hour wind. On each landing the frail landing-gear struts and the old wheels must stand fast with the strain of that twenty-three hundred pounds coming hard down at sixty miles per hour onto the earth, with its mounds and hollows that keep the force from being smooth. I have only to sit within the cockpit and steer, and even this I do while paying only half attention to the job. The other half of the attention is spent ducking forward out of the wind that keeps us in flight, turning imaginary cranks to keep warm, considering other times, other flights, other airplanes.

The least, the very least that I can do in atonement is to see to the needs of my airplane before moving selfishly after my own comfort. Were I not at least to care for her during the time that her wheels are on the ground, I would never have the right to ask a special favor of her, now and then, as she flies. The favor, perhaps, of running on though the rain is in solid walls over her engine, or of wires and struts holding fast in the sudden and furious downdrafts of the mountain winds. And perhaps the ultimate favor of tearing herself to shreds on the rocks of a desert forced landing and allowing her pilot to walk away untouched.

Stopping to think, stopping to analyze as I give her to drink of eighty-octane, I should be able to look with surprise upon myself, and scoff. Asking a favor of an airplane? Letting an airplane get to know you? You feeling all right? But it doesn't work, I can't scoff. I'm not living a fantasy; this is quite solid concrete on the quite solid earth of Augusta, Georgia; in my right glove is the hard steel of a fuel-hose nozzle, with gasoline pouring from it down into a very real fuel tank, and the sharp acid vapor of gasoline flooding over me from the tank as I peer past the nozzle to see how much more fuel the tank will hold. Below me the line boy is punching a sharp metal spout into a metal can of engine oil; the cutting scrape of the spout is quick and harsh and it sounds real enough. This doesn't seem to be a fantasy world, and if it is, it is at least the same familiar fantasy world that I've moved through for several years. Strange, that I should not be able to scoff. When I began to fly, I could have scoffed. After flying ten years and two thousand hours, one should be expected to know some of the realities about flying and about airplanes, and not to dwell in fantasy lands.

It comes with a jolt and with a bit of a shock. Perhaps I *am* beginning to know some of the realities, and those realities include something about getting to know an airplane and letting her get to know you. Perhaps it is true that a pilot's longevity depends sometimes as much upon his faith in his airplane as upon his knowledge of it, and perhaps sometimes the answer to flight isn't always found in wingspans and engine horsepower and resultants of forces plotted on engineering graph paper. And perhaps again I'm wrong. But, right or wrong, I stand and I fuel my own airplane for reasons that seem true and good to me. When the propeller stops in flight over a desert, with rocks around as far as I can see, I'll have the chance to see whether or not I should have scoffed, that morning in Augusta.

## 6

There is a sign by the telephone:

FOR FLIGHT SERVICE, CHECK THE LINE CLEAR, PRESS BLACK
BUTTON TWO SHORT RINGS, SAY "FLIGHT SERVICE, AUGUSTA
MUNICIPAL AIRPORT."

There are thousands of these telephones in airports across the
country, and each one has its own sign with precise directions
for use. It used to be, in aviation, that a pilot could get along
without any directions at all. Press black button for two short
rings.

"Flight Service."

"Hi, Flight Service. Going Augusta on out around Columbus, Auburn-Jackson-Vicksburg. What you got for weather?"
I remember the advice an airline captain once gave me. Never

listen to a weatherman's forecast. The weather that's *there* is the stuff you fly through, and you'll never know what that's like till you get there.

"Looks like a good day. Columbus is clear and twelve miles visibility, Jackson is clear and twenty, Vicksburg clear and twenty. Dallas is clear and fifty, if you want that. Forecast will be for scattered cumulus on into the afternoon, maybe some scattered showers or thundershowers."

"Any winds, surface to five thousand feet?" I wait in interest, consuming a potato-chip breakfast and a bottle of Pepsi-Cola.

"Ah, let's see. Surface winds light and variable through Columbus, going west at ten by the time you get into Jackson-Vicksburg. Five-thousand-foot winds are three three zero degrees fifteen knots, all the way. Looks like it will be a good day."

"Good. Thanks for the weather."

"Can I have your aircraft number?"

"Four nine nine Hotel."

"OK. You want to file a flight plan?"

"Might be nice, but I'm a no-radio airplane."

He laughs, as though I had made some sort of mildly funny joke: an airplane with no radio. "Well then, guess there's not too much we can do for you. . . ."

"Guess not. Thanks for the weather."

Ten minutes from the moment that the telephone touches the cradle near the black button and its list of directions, a biplane is airborne once again over Georgia, flying west. The chill in the air is now a comfortable chill, and not cold. Even without Flight Service doing anything for me, it is fun to be flying. Winds from the west at altitude; those will be head-winds, and those we can do without.

We stay as low as we can, still keeping within gliding range

[63]

of fields fit for landing. At times this is not very low, for the fields are scattered, intruders in the kingdom of pines that mat the earth as far as I can see. Here a road cutting through to parallel my railroad track, here a small lake and pasture, then the pines again, all around. They are old green, dark green, and among them the fresh young lime green of the leaved trees turning early to the sun, looking at it still in wonder. So many trees, so very many trees.

Along the side of a dirt road, a weathered house, a tangled yard. The shadow of the biplane flicks over its chimney and the engine noise must be loud and unusual. No door opens, though, no sign of movement. Now it is gone, and lost behind.

Who lives in the house? What memories does it have tucked into its wood; what happiness has it seen, what joys and what defeats? A full world of life, there, and sorrow and pleasure and gain and loss and interest and bright things happening day on day as the sun rises over the same pines to the east and sets over the same pines to the west. A whole world of important things happening, to real people. Perhaps tomorrow night there is a dance in Marysville, and inside the house there are gingham dresses being ironed. Perhaps a decision made to leave the house and seek a better living in Augusta or Clairmont. Perhaps and perhaps and perhaps. Perhaps there is no one in the house, and it is the body of a house, only. Whatever it is, whatever its story, it took the shadow of the biplane something less than half a second to cross it, and leave it dwindling away behind.

Come, now. Let's stay awake on our navigation. Where are we, by the way? How many miles out from Augusta and how many miles left to go into Auburn? How's that groundspeed? What's our estimate over the next checkpoint? What *is* the next checkpoint? Do I even know our next checkpoint?

Listen to all those old questions. They used to be such important questions, too. Now, in the biplane, they don't matter at all. The question of finding a destination was solved before we took off; there is three hours flying to Auburn, I have five hours of fuel. I follow a railroad track. End navigation problem. At one time away off in the future it was a great game to compute estimates and groundspeeds and to tell to the second when the wheels would touch at destination. But that was with a different sort of airplane and in a world where answers were important things. Miss the estimate and a host of other airplanes would have to be advised. When fuel was critical, and gallons of it burned in a minute, one kept a close watch upon headwinds and groundspeeds. A headwind too strong meant that there wasn't enough fuel to reach destination and one had to land short to refuel. Critical, critical, every bit of it.

Now, in 1929, what matter? With headwinds, I'll arrive a half-hour later, or an hour later, with still an hour's flying left in the tank. I am not in a hurry, for anyone who flies an old slow biplane cannot afford to be in a hurry. What matter if I do not make it to destination? I'll land sooner, at a different destination, and in the next flight pass over my first goal, to another beyond. In 1929, without radio or navigation equipment or an anxious agency waiting my arrival, I am on my own. Seeing a smooth pasture, I can land and take time without worry, and perhaps even trade a ten-minute flight for a homecooked meal.

I know roughly where I am. The sun rises in the east and it sets in the west; I need only follow the setting sun, without ever glancing at a map, and in time I will reach the other coast of the United States. Any town of size has an airport and fuel. Climb, then, when the fuel is getting low, find the town, fill the tank and go on into the west.

The biplane rachets and thunders through the low sky, brightwinged, whirring, pulling a shadow ninety miles per hour across the sandy earth and through the needled treetops. Things moving, things to watch, air to drink and to slice into long ribbons with wingwires. But still the strange touch of the dream so long dreamed.

Perhaps in a few thousand years flight will become something we can accept and believe to be real. Do the gulls enjoy flying, and the hawks? Probably not. Probably they wish that they could stride along the ground, and know what it is to be held firmly down and not subject to every toss of an air current. I'd like to say, "I'll trade you, hawk," but I'd want to attach a few strings to the deal. The more I consider it, the more strings there would be to attach, until in the end I'd only want to be me, with an ability to fly. And this is what I am at this moment. I'll still take my life and my clumsy clattery way of moving through the air. For in working and striving and sacrificing for this way of flying, I can enjoy it fully; give me flight without effort and I'll turn shortly, bored, to something that challenges.

A challenge: let us invent a way that will allow us to fly. And poor earthbound man sought and dreamed and worked for a long time before he struck upon an answer. Try wings like the birds' wings, try sails like a boat's, try the flame of gunpowder rockets. Try and try and try. Kites and cloth and feathers and wood and steam engines, nets about birds and frames of bamboo. Then bamboo with cloth stretched and a cradle for the man pilot. If I build a mountain and stretch my bamboo wings at the top, and run down the side of the mountain into the wind . . . and there he had it. Man at last was flying. Months of flights from the mountaintop, but still, it should be able to last longer, I should be able to taste more fully this rare sweetness. Oars, then, and pedals and treadmills and handcranks and paddlewheels and flapping wings and a little homebuilt gasoline engine. If we take the engine, and attach a chain drive that can turn two propellers and fit it all to the wings and perhaps the pilot can lie down on the lower wing . . . Another step made, another beginning. A beginning laid down for all mankind to work from.

At first, flying is a blind sort of fun, the challenge again, something different to do. Enjoyable to feel in control of a big metallic bird and look down on all the little buildings and lakes and ants on the road. In time, for those who persevere through the archaic accumulation of tests that lead to a pilot's license, the joy subtly switches from that of controlling the bird into that of being the bird, with eyes bright for looking down, with wings that on the ground are only wood and cloth and sheet aluminum, but in flight become so alive that one can feel feathers in the wind.

We notice first the change in the world outside us. It changes from familiar low perspective to the unfamiliar high one, and we wonder what it would feel like to fall all that way down. Fun it might be, but a timid kind of fun, for after all, we say, the air is not really our element. We don't change our mind about that for a long time.

Then come the hours when we feel uneasily at home, with time to notice the world again, when the flying takes care of itself. From this the uneasiness goes out, as we learn that we can handle many problems successfully.

And then we begin to see the earth and the sky as symbols. The mountain is not so much a mass of peaked earth to be feared as an obstacle to be conquered in pursuit of a higher goal.

And an airplane, we discover, is a teacher. A calm, subtle, persuasive teacher, for it is infinitely patient. An airplane does not question its pilot's motives, or misunderstand him, or have

[67]

hurt feelings for him to soothe. Like the sky, an airplane simply *is*, offering its lessons. If we wish to learn the lessons, they are there in plenty, and can become very detailed and profound lessons.

Columbus ahead. A touch backward on the control stick to lift us from the treetops to a platform high above them. One is not allowed to cross cities at low altitude and one should not, even if there were no law. Cities do not offer many good places to land if an engine should stop, and those not interested in airplanes should not have their thought turned for an instant by the sound of cylinders firing to blur a propeller. Two thousand feet, then, over Columbus, and the flight goes for a moment less interesting. At low level there is a blurred fringe on the land speeding by. At two thousand feet, the fringe is gone and all is clear and sharp, slow-moving. There the highways leading into the city, and automobiles and trucks crowding along. There a refinery, going to a great amount of effort to the simple end that the smoke from its tall stacks should tell the pilot of a passing biplane from just what direction the wind is blowing. There, on the meadow by the river, is Columbus Municipal Airport, with many runways angled and set for many winds. A curved airplane-parking ramp, and oil spots from its passenger airplanes in front of the terminal. Columbus Municipal Airport is no place for an old radioless biplane.

From the concrete giant, for a second, there shines a green light. There. Again. From the control tower, a brilliant green pencil flashing. And behind the green, a tiny figure in the tower. He is clearing me to land. How kind of him, how very thoughtful! From two thousand feet above his airport, we have been invited to stop and have a cup of coffee and talk about the old days.

Thank you very much, friend, but I must really be on my

[68]

way. Wouldn't want to disturb those airplanes that do believe in radios. We rock our wings in thanks, and rock them with a gentle wish, for his is an unusual offer. There is an interesting fellow behind the green light at Columbus Municipal, and someday I shall come through here again and ask of him.

A crossing of a river, some tall radio towers sliding below, and the country closes back in as the city has gone. Cities are always losing the battle. No matter how big they are, there is always the country; patient, like a quiet green sea about it, waiting to close back in. The ground changes quickly from Modern back to Always, after one flies over a city. A strip of motels hangs on for a moment lining the highways into town, but at last they surrender and the country takes over, and with it the quiet life and the quiet people. Again the roar of the engine drifts down to treetop height and is absorbed into green needles.

Parallel to the deserted road that will bring me to the Auburn airport is a wide field cut, and level, fit for landing. My money in the bank, that allows me play and the enjoyment of flying low.

Two tall pines ahead, a wingspan apart, swifting closer, stretching high above us until one last second and hard back on the control stick and full left aileron and in a steep climbing turn we watch the needles brush by. That's the consciousness of flying, when you can reach out and touch the ground moving by, and brush the branches of a tree as you pass. There is no place that is more fun to fly than a horizon-to-horizon meadow with trees sparsely planted. Fly down low with wheels flicking through the grass; flash by the first trees at cow-level so that they look normal and unscalable, rush toward the next that look just as haughty and then in a simple small movement of stick and rudder roar straight up and over and roll inverted and look down at its branches.

[69]

Yet how they worked, how those first to fly worked to get away from the ground! Years of their life and thought for a flight of a hundred feet, for an altitude of ten feet, for twenty seconds in the air. And today we can taste the sheer and untrammeled fun of flying the twenty seconds, then another twenty, and another. Roll the wheels in the meadow, swing them high and rolling over the top of the tallest trees. Slice the rush of air with a wingtip, with a glove, with eyes squinting. This is flying. The power to throw yourself happily through the sky, to see the familiar world from any angle at all, or not to see it, to turn one's head and spend an hour in the otherworld of the hills and plains and cliffs and lakes and meadows all built of cloud.

But take a pilot in his very favorite airplane and immerse him in his very favorite conditions: meadow with trees planted, mountains to conquer, alone in the sunset clouds. Rarely, very rarely, and then only if you watch very closely, you may see him smile. I caught myself at this and asked how could it be.

It was low-level flying over the desert, at very high speed, leading a flight of four F-86 Sabrejets to a target. All the cards were there and face up: we needed the low-level training mission to fill a squadron requirement; we were heavy on fuel and had to go full throttle to burn it away; the ground was flat and the air was caught in the stillness of early morning. At the end of the low-level flight waited the gunnery targets. I flew a good airplane, and the bet was a nickel for every bullet hole in the target.

Result, then, was a needle on the airspeed indicator that settled on 540 miles per hour. Result was the need for tiny little movements of the control stick to follow the low rise and fall of the earth and for quick jumps over tall cactus. Result was three friends in loose formation to left and right, engaging all in the favorite mission of highspeed low-level, and a challenge waiting. Eight heavy machine guns, in that flight, loaded and ready to fire. Four smooth sweptwing arrows that were sheer beauty in their silver against the early desert, one rising here over a boulder, one dipping now into a hollow, banking sharply to avoid a single yucca plant. Like kids down the block playing at Jet Fighter Pilot, with great big pretty authentic official toys, splitting the air with sudden howitzer-sounds to the lizards in the sun, and not a single human ear to be disturbed or to voice complaint.

Speed and power and control; toys enjoyed to their fullest. But I wasn't smiling. I wasted a precious second of that joy distilled in concern. Why wasn't I smiling? I should be laughing, singing, were there room to dance I should be dancing.

The lesson then, handed from a different airplane, handed at a speed of 543 miles per hour, at an altitude of seven feet three inches. Inwardly, inwardly, pilot. The only important things happen within yourself. Something great and wild and different and unusual may happen outside of you, but the meaning and importance of it come from within. A smile is outward, a way of communicating. Here you can be lost in the joy and hold it all to yourself, knowing it, tasting it, feeling it, being happy. No communication required.

There, beyond the powerlines, Auburn airport. Back on the stick, roaring up over the wires, seeing clearly and at once the two hard-surface runways, the two grass landing strips, a scarlet windsock stirring softly above the gasoline pumps. Into the wind, circle the field, pick the landing strip and the part of the strip that we shall land upon. The parachute is hard; it will be good to get out and walk around. One lonely biplane in the landing pattern, but the biplane is not aware of

[73]

her loneliness and turns easily toward the bright spring grass.

A good strip, this, not even the ruts of many landings worn into it. An inviting soft place to come again to ground and a place that the biplane can turn toward as she has so many times before. Throttle back and the propeller becomes a silent windmill. Down we glide, green ahead, wind going soft in the wires, whishing gently just enough to say that it is there. Forward on the stick, forward and the trees growing tall at each side of the strip, and taller and the grass is blocked out ahead and blurred to the sides, stick back now, as we slow, and back and back . . . and with a little crash we're down and rolling on all three wheels, clattering and thudding through the unevenness from which the green grows. Left-rudder-right-rudder and here we are all of a sudden at that familiar speed at which I could hop over the side and walk. A touch of throttle and we taxi slowly toward the gasoline pumps and the few buildings clustered around. Neither old buildings nor new; one a hangar, another a flight school with windows looking out upon the runways, another hangar around back. A few people standing near the door, talking and watching the biplane as it taxies.

A burst of power and the pulsing wind beating back upon me for a moment, then left rudder to swing around near the low-octane pump and bring the red-knobbed mixture lever forward to *Idle-Cutoff*. The engine runs on for four seconds, then all at once it goes quiet and I can hear the pistons clanking softly and the propeller coasting to a stop.

Switch off.

Fuel off.

Seat belt unfastened, parachute straps unbuckled, gloves off, helmet off and feel the gentle soft wind that doesn't come from a propeller. Still sunlight. Quiet. I can have only a nodding acquaintance with the quiet, for the engine roars on in my ears; the ghost engine, the spirit of a thing that one might be tempted to call dead.

The little crowd walks over as I begin to refill the tank. They are awed a bit and look silently at the old airplane. Flight students, and they do not see many old airplanes flying. Are they aware of the biplane as a heritage, or just as a strange relic that has come wandering through? It would be good to know, but one can't ask a stranger group are you aware of this as a heritage. One can't ask that sort of a thing until one gets to know them, until they are strangers no more.

"Hi. Any place around here to get a sandwich?"

## 7

THE BIPLANE FLIES on, following the road west to incidents, to lessons. From small incidents, like the filling of a gasoline tank; from bigger incidents, like the spinning crash on the runway at Crescent Beach, something to learn and to apply to knowledge and future action.

The land changes subtly, the pines cut back for more and more farms to lay themselves green on the earth, under the sun. Like the Land of Oz it is becoming, and the road I follow might as well be of yellow brick. So very neat is the land, even from a short hundred feet in the air. There isn't a grassblade out of place in the pastures, even the cows are standing over X's chalked on the ground by a careful director. Places, everyone! Places! Action! Roll 'em!

I feel like an intruder over the set, and the engine noise will ruin the sound man's tapes. Somewhere around here, under a giant oak, must be a sound man and a boom mike. But wait. We're part of the show. And right on cue:

Enter BIPLANE, flying east to west. Sound of BIPLANE rises from TINY WHISPER to ROAR overhead to fade into WHIS-PER in west. CUT to cockpit of BIPLANE. Camera holds for moment on COWS, pans forward along YELLOW BRICK ROAD, pans out to FARMHOUSE. *Note to Property Manager:* FARM-HOUSE should symbolize EMERALD CITY; symbolize neatness, spotlessness, everything in working order and moving peacefully through time, should suggest that the over-rainbow magic city often takes forms that we know best, so we cannot see the magic existing.
CUT to GIANT OAK, from whose shade we watch BIPLANE approaching again east to west, passing LOUD and ROARING through leaves overhead, dwindling and finally disappearing in the west. Dissolve to black and green letters: THE END.

Good take! Print it!

Nice that it went so well, but for the biplane, the show is still going on, and on and on. Beneath us, hundreds of directors working hidden, from canvas-backed chairs. Places! Action! BIPLANE. FARMHOUSE. EMERALD CITY. And through it all, YELLOW BRICK ROAD. This is the South in spring, 1929. Every once in a while, some children by their Saturday stream, waving, and worthy of a wave back, from a hundred feet away. And gone. People living down there. I can see them living and fishing and swimming and plowing and starting fires that lift blue smoke up through chimneys. Smoke that curls and drifts in the wind and tells me that the headwind has come now down to the ground. Not a strong wind, but enough to keep us from moving quite so quickly as we would across the earth. And the slower we fly, the more we see the earth and appreciate it. An airplane, especially an antique airplane, cannot hurry. It has only one

[77]

working speed. For the biplane, I set the throttle in level flight until the tachometer needle steadies at 1725 revolutions. A good comfortable speed where the engine sounds right, neither loafing nor straining; 1725 becomes a good sound, a right sound in the wind. In still air, 1725 gives something like ninety-five miles per hour; in the headwind this noon we move eighty miles per hour across the ground. We definitely will not startle the country with a new speed record on this crossing.

But we do startle ourselves with a sight of a beautiful land wheeling below. The South is supposed to be an ugly place, and on occasion, on the ground, I have seen it ugly, twisted and roiled in blind dull hatred. But from the air one cannot see hatred roiling and the South is a place with gentleness and beauty filled.

Airplanes offer pilots a balance for evil, and more than one pilot, more than ten, keeps in his mind an index of places he has seen from the air that are good. In my own file is a valley in the hills bordering the sea at Laguna Beach, California. And that valley just to the east of Salt Lake City, Utah, on the other side of the big mountain there, where down the valley a river flows and in summer it is Shangri-La perfected. There is a good place in eastern Pennsylvania, that happens even to have a little grass airstrip near it. An airline pilot told me of a place he discovered in Arizona. He had seen it from thirty-two thousand feet on the New York–Los Angeles run, had studied it on every flight since his discovery. He said it would be a good place to go, when he retires, to be alone and quiet.

There is a plain in northern France, a hill in Germany, a beach of sand like sugar on the Gulf side of Florida. And today I add another to my file: the farms and the pastures of central Alabama. If a need comes for escape, these are waiting.

Places that are good. And, too, times that are good. Not

[78]

*have been* good. Are good. For they remain, and I can savor their goodness by simply opening the file and picking one out and refeeling the thought that came from the incident. Not the incident that matters, but the learning. Not the symbol, but its meaning. Not the outside, but what happens within.

Pick a card, any card. Here is one; at the top it is marked *Pat and Lou—El Toro*. An incident.

I had been away from the 141st Tactical Fighter Squadron for a year, moved to the other side of the country from them. And one day a phone call. Patrick Flanagan and Lou Pisane, Crosscountry Aces of the New Jersey Air National Guard, scoring again. This time they were on a 2600-mile training mission, and had landed their F-86's at El Toro Marine Air Station, thirty miles from me.

The card is written and filled with old days renewed, of the time Pat managed with a clumsy old F-84F to outfox a Royal Canadian Air Force Mark VI Sabre in the skies of France, to track him for a moment in his gunsight. A mock battle, of course, yet the Mark VI was an airplane built for air combat and the 84 was not. But Pat is a skillful pilot, and with just a little embellishing here and there and with a polished gift of the dramatic and the funny, why, the poor Maple Leaf didn't have a chance from the beginning.

And Lou; tall cool Lou, who taught me something about patience as I flew his wing one day and he stalked and finally caught a French fighter plane, to make a roaring blasting pass a yard off his wingtip to remind him that one must look around or he will be caught even by old F-84's. Lou, as formal and polite and absolutely proper as though he had been raised on etiquette from the moment he could listen; till you got to know him and he came alive, cool still, but a sharp logical mind that wouldn't stand for nonsense even from the commanding general. "Aw c'mon, General. You know and I

[79]

know we don't read every single item on that checklist in the Preflight. If you want us to carry the checklist around in our hand while we make the Preflight, just say so. But don't try to give us that stuff about reading every single item on there every single time we go out to fly."

Filed under Times that are Good, to see them again and to drive them back to the flight line at El Toro. And there, surrounded by Marine airplanes, two silver Air Guard F-86's parked together.

"Kinda sad to leave the 84's in France, but the 86 is a good airplane too, and before long the squadron will be getting 105's. Don't you wish you were back with us?"

"Back with you characters? I had to go clear across the country to get away from you guys, and now you follow me out here, even. Good old 86. Mind if I look in your cockpit, Lou, if I promise not to touch any switches? Boy, there aren't enough wild horses left in this world to drive me back into the 141st Tac Fighter Squadron."

Look at that cockpit. Everything there, the way it used to be: armament panel, throttle, speed brake switch, flight instruments, the long-handled landing-gear switch, circuit breaker panels, the pins in the ejection seat. You guys never learn anything, a dangerous bunch to be with. "Lou, you left your checklist up here! How can you run a proper Preflight inspection without that checklist in your hand?" Never obey regulations. A hopeless bunch.

And the time is come for a last handshake in the dusk as they climb up the kicksteps to their cockpits, and strap in. The strange uncomfortable feeling that I've got to hurry to get into my airplane, or they'll take off without me. Where's my airplane? I've never had to stay on the ground while the rest of my flight makes ready to go. His helmet and oxygen mask fitted now, Pat talks for a moment on the radio, copying the instrument departure clearance in his high cockpit, reading it back to the control tower. Hey, Pat! Remember the time when Roj Schmitt was on your wing, his first time up in the weather? And he said, "Don't worry about me, just fly it like you're alone. . . ." Do you remember, Pat?

Hey, Lou! Remember back in Chaumont when you bet that the shock of a parachute landing was no more than you'd get if you jumped out a two-story window? Remember?

And Pat draws the start-engine circle in the air to Lou, and, darn it, he draws it to me too, standing on the ramp, in a civilian business suit. Why did you do that, Flanagan? You hoop, you darn silly hoop. And FOOM-FOOM! the two engines burst together into life, the rising whine of the compressors sucking air in the intake and the rumble of the combustion chambers turning it into fire and pushing it through the turbine. I can shout now and they'll only see my mouth moving. There the wheels start to roll, and they turn to taxi by me on the way to the runway. Hidden dust sprays out of the concrete where the jetblast catches it in a scorching storm. Pat taxies by, way up in his cockpit, looking down at me, tossing a little salute. See ya, Pat. See ya round, boy. His wingtip grazes my suit coat, the high-swept rudder sails proudly by. And twenty feet behind comes Lou, breaking regulations. You're supposed to have a hundred feet separation when you taxi, Pisane. Think you're at some kind of an air show, ace?

A salute from the cockpit, returned from a civilian in a business suit, standing on the concrete. Give the general hell for me, Lou. Not that you wouldn't, anyway.

And they're gone down the taxiway, as the blue taxilights come on in the evening. Way down at the end of the runway there's a thunderstorm of two airplanes running up their engines. What are you doing right now, Pat? Emergency fuel check? Stomp on those brakes, run the throttle up to 95 percent rpm, reach over and throw in the emergency fuel switch, let the rpm stabilize, run it on up to full throttle, cut the power back and switch over to normal fuel. And Lou? Checks done, run her up to 98 percent, hold the brakes, nod across to Pat when you're ready to roll.

The tiny little fighters at the end of the runway begin to move, trailing thin black smoke of full throttle. Together they grow, lift from the ground, together gear doors drop open, landing gear sucks back into two smooth fuselages, gear doors close, stiff and robotlike. Faster and faster they move, flying low in the air.

Locked in tight formation, they're suddenly fire-eating arrows overhead, trying to blast the air loose with sheer sound and fury, and send it in avalanche to the runway. For one long proud moment they're in side silhouette, and from the ground I can see the dots of the pilots in the cockpits. Then I see wings only, and rudders and elevators and two trails of thin black smoke.

They grow smaller and smaller toward the mountains in the east, climbing now, swiftly . . . and smaller . . . goodbye, Pat . . . and smaller . . . tuck it in there, Lou-babe . . . and gone.

Two trails of smoke in the air, twisting now in the wind.

I look down in the dead quiet to see my civilian shoes standing on the damned concrete and I can't see shoes or concrete very clearly and it's just as damn well because even with the damn floodlights on, the night comes in and blurs things. Why did you have to come back, you guys? Why'd you follow me, then leave without me, you blockheads? You hoops couldn't get me back in that damn squadron for all the damn tea in China.

Lots of times filed away, in that box, lots of incidents.

[82]

Shadows on the ground. Not long ones. Indicators only that the sun is passing me by. Inevitable, I guess. If the sun moved eighty miles an hour around the earth we'd have a pretty long day. Go on ahead, sun. About time for me to land, anyway. I can get one more hop in today; might make it to the Mississippi, with luck.

The clean clipped pastures of Oz have given way to a swampy land, and still lakes lying warm. The biplane pulls her shadow steadily along, driving it down the road to slowly slowly pass an occasional automobile. Thank heaven we're still passing the cars. There's the cutoff point between Fast and Slow. As long as you can pass the cars, you've got nothing to worry about.

Ahead, what is a thin blue circle on the map becomes Demopolis, Alabama. Not far from a river (squiggly blue on the map), ground covered nearby with reeds. A great big giant airport, in the precise and geometrical center of Nowhere. Even the town of Demopolis is a long drive down the road. During the war, the airport must have trained some kind of aviator, but now it is nearly deserted, with one tiny gasoline pump, one solitary windsock, a weathered building nearby. Down again on the grass, airplane, and into the wind, to see what we shall find.

We shall find, strangely, a little crowd of people, appearing from hidden nowhere to see the biplane. She is an Event at Demopolis, where there is only one other airplane parked in sight, on fifty acres of concrete and two hundred acres of airport surrounding. Questions in the sun, while the fuel hoses softly into the tank.

"Where you from?"

"North Carolina."

"Where you goin'?"

"Los Angeles."

A pause. A look inside the cockpit, at the little black instrument panel. "That's a long way."

"It does seem a long way." And I think of the gallons of gasoline I still have to pump into this tank, and of the hours yet to peer around the oilsmeared windscreen, of the sun at my back in the mornings to come, and in my eyes in the evenings. It does seem a long way to go.

Inside the flight office, and time enough for a bottle of eternal Pepsi-Cola. I know that it must be very quiet here, but the engine is still firing 1–3–5–2–4 in my ears. One more flight today. Stretch one long flight, fly till the sun goes down. Perhaps the Mississippi tonight. Good to stand up, to be able to walk around. Been in the cockpit a long time today. Be nice just to stretch out on the grass and go to sleep. One more hop and I'll do it.

# 8

It's all beginning to fade, and run together. I catch myself seeking to hurry. Trees growing back and crowding in about the road and as far as I can see there are treetops greening in the afternoon. There have been many hours spent this day in this cockpit, and I am tired.

Instantly, an astonished little voice. Tired? Tired of flying? Oho, so all it takes is a few hours of the wind and you're tired, ready to quit. We see at last there is a difference between the pilots of then and of now. Not even halfway across and you're breaking under the tiny strain of a few hours' flying.

All right, that's enough of that. You've not much evidence to prove that the early pilots didn't get tired, and you'll note that I had no thoughts of quitting, or even of slowing down.

Not words, but action will decide whether I can stand with them. Only by living it can I discover flight.

So it is that many people travel by airplane, but few know what it is to fly. A passenger waiting in an airline terminal sees the airplanes through a twenty-foot sheet of glass, from an air-conditioned cube in which soft music plays. The sound of an engine is a muffled murmur outside, a momentary purring background for the music. In some terminals the reality is almost served to them on a silver tray, for their clothes can be whipped by the same propellerblast, that same sacred propellerblast, that whipped the coats of the great men of flight. And the airplane is right there, towering over them, that has flown many hours and will fly many more before it is replaced by one more modern. So often, though, the propellerblast is only a force that tugs at one's lapels, an annoyance; and the big airplanes are barely noticed by passengers who are concerned only with finding the entry steps as quickly as possible, to escape the wind. And the airplane, with so much to offer those who will only take the time to see, does it go unseen? The curve of its wing, that has changed the history and the highway of mankind, is it unnoticed?

Well, what do you know. Not unnoticed. There in the wind, hands in pockets, hunched against the sunny cold, the first officer, three gold stripes on his sleeves, paying no attention to the passengers, pays full attention to his airplane. He sees that there are no leaks in the hydraulic lines, that everything is neat and in order inside the giant wheel wells of the wing. The wheels themselves, and the tires, all look good. On around the airplane he walks, looking at it, checking it, enjoying it without a trace of a smile.

The picture is complete. The passengers find their cushioned seats, and will soon be on their way in a machine that so many neither understand nor care to understand. The first

[86]

officer and the captain do understand, and care for their airplane, and pay her every attention. So no one is forgotten; the airplane is happy, and the flight crew, and the passengers are ready to go their way.

Still, one airplane is two very separate places. In the passenger cabin, the fear that this may be the Last Flight, the awareness of air crashes in newspaper headlines, a certain tension in the narrow air when the throttles come forward, and a hoping that there will be one more flight safely completed before the next set of headlines are splashed across the newsstands. Step forward, through the door and onto the flight deck, and tension disappears as though there were no such thing. The captain in the left seat, the first officer in the right, the flight engineer at his board of solid instruments behind the first officer. All is smooth routine, for it has been lived many times over and again. Throttles come forward all under one hand, checks and crosschecks of engine instruments and of airspeed slowly increasing, a hand on the nosewheel steering shifts to the control column when the flight controls become effective before the airplane is off the ground. The voice of the first officer, as he reads the airspeed indicator: "V-one." A little code that means, "Captain, we are committed to fly; there is not enough room left to stop the airplane without rolling off the end of the runway."

"V-R." And in the captain's hand the control wheel comes back slightly, and the nosewheel lifts from the ground. A tiny pause, and mainwheels come free and the airplane is flying. A hand, the first officer's, on the switch marked *Landing Gear— Up*, and a rumbling sheathing sound from the depths of the airplane as the gigantic heavy wheels, still spinning, move ponderously up into the wheel wells.

"V-two." Or, "At this airspeed, we can lose an engine and still be able to climb." The takeoff is marked by checkpoints

[87]

saying, this is what we can do if we lose an engine now. Takeoff is the beginning, for the flight crew, of an interesting time with many little problems to solve. They are real problems, but they are not difficult, and they are the kind of problems that flight crews solve every hour, every flight. What is the estimated time of arrival over Ambrose intersection? Get a position report ready for Phoenix Center as we cross Winslow, give them a call on the number two radio, on frequency 126.7 megacycles. Transmit a report to the weather stations, telling the actual winds along our course and the turbulence and cloud tops and any icing along the way. Steer 236 degrees for a while, then add three degrees, settle on 239 degrees to correct for the winds.

Little problems, familiar ones, and friendly. Once in a while a bigger problem will come along, but that is part of the fun and keeps flying a fresh and a good way to make a living. If only the door to the passenger cabin from the flight deck weren't such an effective door, the confidence and the interest that come from thousands of flying hours might filter back and destroy the tension and the fear that there exists.

As it is, even airline pilots are often uneasy when they must fly as passengers. Each pilot would feel a little more comfortable if he were at the controls and not sitting to look at a faceless door that doesn't admit that there is anyone at all on the flight deck. Gone for pilots is the fun of flying as passenger, unknowing and fearful, unknowing and enjoying flight. There is always the creature within that is criticizing the way an airplane is being flown. Even sitting at the rear of a 110-passenger jetliner there is one lonely soul, during landing, that is saying wordlessly to the pilot, "Not now, you fool! We're rounding out too soon! East it forward, ease it on in . . . that's the way . . . too much, too much! Pull it back now! Flare out or you'll . . ." and with a thump the wheels are rolling on the concrete. "Well, all right," from the back of the passenger cabin, "but *I* could have had her down much more smoothly."

The biplane hums loudly along with the sun now low ahead, a round circle of distorted oily brightness in the forward windscreen. Not much daylight left to fly. The baseball sun, thrown high, having paused at its noon top, comes whistling down through the horizon. Though the sky goes on being happily light, the ground is not taken in. The ground is a solemn keeper of very precise time, and when the sun is down it dutifully smothers its dwellers in darkness.

Vicksburg below, and there, with shadows half across its opaque brown waves, the Mississippi. A river barge, a bridge that is probably a toll bridge, and on it automobiles, and among the automobiles a sparkling of headlights coming on. Time to land, and a few miles south is the airport for Vicksburg. But the map says that there are two airports close ahead westward; if I can land at one of these I can be that much farther along my course when the sun begins its launch tomorrow.

Press on, the voice says. If you don't find the airports you can land in a field, and find fuel farther on in the morning. The voice that speaks is the one within that always seeks adventure, and, living only for adventure, doesn't care what happens to aircraft or pilot. Tonight, once again, it wins its case. We leave the Mississippi and Vicksburg behind, and press on. Louisiana rolls onto the map.

The land is all cut into dark squares, in which are probably growing green peppers and peas that have black eyes. And on one square grows a cluster of wooden buildings. A town. There should be an airport here, but I can see no sign of one. It is there, of course, somewhere, but little airports can be

[89]

impossible to find even in broad daylight. "Airport" is often just a word applied to a pasture, to the side of which a farmer keeps a camouflaged fuel pump. It is a recognized game and point of competition in some parts of the country: Find the Airport. Pick one of the thin blue circles on an aeronautical map, one that no player has ever seen before. Take off at five-minute intervals to find it. The winners, those that find the airport, share a week of superiority over those who may be directly overhead, yet unseeing. "That can never happen to me," I remember saying, when first a friend suggested we play Find the Airport. "What a silly game." But in gracious tolerance I condescended to race him to the airport.

I spent the better part of that afternoon circling above the many-pastured countryside, searching and searching, combing every single pasture, and there were many, before my wife finally saw an airplane parked on the grass and we shakily completed the game. A very official airport, too. Under the trees were not one, but two gas pumps waiting, and a row of small hangars, a restaurant, a swimming pool.

So this evening, west of the Mississippi, I do not even bother to circle. I will seek the one next airport, and, failing to find that, will land in a field and wait for the daylight.

The trees are cut far back from the road here, wide farmlands broad to each side, and farmhouses with lights coming on inside. A lonely feeling, watching those lights come on.

Ahead, a town, Rayville, Louisiana. Just to the west should be the airport. And obviously, clearly, there it is. A single narrow strip of asphalt, a short row of open hangars, a lone and tattered windsock. Crosswind. Hard surface and cross-wind. But a gentle one; it couldn't be more than five miles per hour. Surely THAT isn't enough to pose a problem. The crosswind lesson has been a bitter one, one not easily for-

[90]

gotten, but it is going dark on the ground and I must make my decision quickly. If I do not land here, I must pick my field, and a good field will be difficult to choose in the shadows and I will still need the fuel in the morning. It would be good to land at Rayville. So near, only a thousand feet away from me. Yet, with the crosswind, a thousand feet is a long way away. A low pass certainly won't hurt, one of the many voices within has suggested. And truly. Nothing to be lost by a low pass down the runway, except possibly a few minutes.

So into the pattern we go and slide down the invisible ramp of air that leads to the end of every runway ever built. Across the fence, ten feet high. Five feet. It is not good. The biplane has to crab into the wind in order to fly straight down the runway; to land like this would be a very risky thing at best. And look there, pilot. Not thirty feet from the edge of the runway, a long earth embankment paralleling. How high? Two feet? Three feet? High enough; a one-foot embankment would be high enough to shear the landing gear from the biplane were she to run off the narrow runway. And with the crosswind from that direction, that is the way she would turn. If she lost her gear, that would be the end of the story. Propeller and engine would twist and bury themselves into the earth, the lower wing panels rip away and probably take the upper wing with them. There wouldn't be much left. So. Decision?

I must land without hitting the embankment. I'm a good pilot, after all. Haven't I flown almost two thousand hours in many airplanes? I have, and I've flown from zero miles per hour to a shade over twice the speed of sound. Surely, surely I can land an old biplane on a runway with a five-mile crosswind.

Decision made, we're once again down the ramp, this time

[91]

with intent to stop on the ground. Careful, ease it down, let the main wheels touch. Good; forward on the stick to hold those main wheels down and the rudder high in the air. Watch it watch it, she's going to want to swing to the left, into the embankment. Nice touchdown, just a little while longer and we'll be laughing at our fears. Here she comes, tailwheel coming down, now pull hard back on the stick to pin the tail down and hope the tailwheel steering works . . . left rudder, right rudder, full right rudder look OUT BOY SHE'S SWINGING IT'S TOO LATE I CAN'T CONTROL HER WE'RE GOING TO HIT THAT DIRT!

Well, if we're going to hit it, we're going to hit it hard. Full throttle stick forward and maybe we can fly off before the dirt, a chance in a hundred.

WHAT ARE YOU DOING WITH THAT THROTTLE WE'RE GOING TO HIT THE DIRT THERE'S NOTHING YOU CAN DO ABOUT IT LOOK OUT HANG ON HERE WE GO!!

In a second the biplane rolls off the runway, throttle wide open and engine roaring full power, angling sharply toward the dirt wall.

And here, in the space of another second, two people struggling within the pilot. One has given up, is certain that there is to be a big splintering crash in the next instant. The other, thinking still, playing one last card, one very last card, and now, playing, without time even to glance at the airspeed to see if the airplane will fly, slams hard back on the control stick.

The biplane points her nose up, but refuses to fly. The card player is philosophical. We played what we had and we lost. There will be a crashing sound in the next tenth of a second. Pilot, I hope you've learned about crosswinds.

The crash comes, and over the engine roar I can hear it, I

can feel it in the controls. A dull thud at first, as though we had hit something that was very heavy but also very soft, with the left main landing gear. And then—nothing.

We're flying!

We are just barely flying, staggering through the air above the grass over the embankment. One tenth of a second for relief, and another for shock; ahead is a barbed-wire fence and a stand of trees. The embankment would have been better. I'm going to hit those trees in full flight, I don't have a chance of clearing them.

Here, let me have it.

It is the gambler again, taking over.

Nose down, we must put the nose down to gain flying speed. The stick inches forward in my hand, and the wheels roll in the grass. They lift again in a moment and the biplane gathers speed. Here comes the fence, and the gambler waits until the last second, gaining every bit of speed he can. Then back on the stick and the fence is cleared and no time to think a full hard right bank and we flash between two poplars, thirty feet above the ground. For a second the world is green leaves and black branches and then suddenly it is darkening blue sky.

OK, the gambler says offhandedly, you can fly it now. That is a weak hand on the control stick, but a hand that would sooner guide the biplane to landing on the highway into the wind than take another try at the crosswind runway. There must be another place to land.

Another circle of the airport and there it is. Like the prayers of the ancients answered in manna all about them, there comes for me the knowledge that the Rayville Airport has two landing strips, and the other strip is grass and it is facing into the wind. Why didn't I notice it before?

[93]

Five minutes later the airplane is parked by the hangars and I walk along the embankment to see where the left wheel hit the dirt.

How was it possible? Even the gambler had been sure that we were going to hit the dike, and hit it very hard indeed. But we didn't. We grazed it so softly that there is no sign left in the grass. The biplane had no reason to fly then; only a moment before, she was not even moving fast enough to hold her tail in the air. Being a big inanimate object, some would say, the biplane could not have put forth any special effort to fly. Show me aerodynamically, they could say, one single reason for that airplane to fly before it had reached its proper flying speed. And of course I cannot give one single aerodynamic reason. Then, they say, you must have had proper flying speed at the moment you pulled back on the stick. Case closed. What shall we talk about now?

But I walk away unconvinced. I may not be able to land an old biplane in a crosswind, but the other is true: I have flown airplanes for a long enough time to know what to expect from them. If the biplane, in the space of what was at the very most seventy feet, went from twenty miles per hour to full flight, it is the shortest takeoff I have made in any flying machine, save the helicopters. And I have deliberately and very studiously practiced short-field takeoffs in airplanes heavy and light. The shortest I have ever made took some 290 feet of runway and that was wheels-barely-off-the-ground, not clearing a two-foot dike of earth.

My old impossible beliefs have today been reaffirmed. The last answer to flight is not found in the textbooks of aerodynamics. If it were up to aerodynamics, the biplane would at this moment be a cluttered trail of wheels, fuselage and wingpanels angling off the runway at Rayville, Louisiana. But it is not, and stands whole and complete, without a scratch, waiting for whatever adventures will come our way tomorrow.

The clatter of a pickup truck turning onto the gravel drive of the airport. Painted dimly on its door, ADAMS FLYING SERVICE, and behind the wheel a puzzled smile beneath a widebrim Stetson turned up in front, as the Old-Timer always turns up his brim in the western movies.

"Couldn't figure out what you were. Came over the house and I haven't heard an engine sound like that for twenty years. Ran out and looked at you and you were too small to be a Stearman, didn't look quite like a Waco and for sure not a Travel-Air. What the heck kind of airplane is that, anyway?"

"Detroit-Parks. Not too many of them made, so don't feel bad you didn't know her. Wright engine. You should have been able to tell the Wright, way it's all covered with oil."

[95]

"Adams, the name. Lyle. Yeah. Wright stop throwing oil and you better look out. Mind if I look inside?"

Headlights wash the biplane as the pickup turns and rolls closer. The door squeaks open and there are footsteps on the gravel.

"This is a nice little airplane. Look at that. Booster magneto, isn't it? Boy. Haven't seen an airplane with a booster mag since I was a kid. And a spark advance. Hey. This is a real flying machine!"

"Nice to hear those words, sir. Most people look at her and wonder how such an old pile of sticks and rag ever get into the air."

"No, no. Fine airplane. Hey, you want to put her in the hangar tonight? I'll roll one of the Ag-Cats out and we can swing you right on in. Never matter if it rain on the Cat. Throw a cockpit cover on her, is all."

"Why, thank y', Lyle. Doesn't look like we'll be getting any rain tonight, though, and I want to be gone before the sun's up tomorrow. Kinda hard to pull out of a hangar for one guy to do. We been sleeping out anyway."

"Suit yourself. But I start dusting about sunup anyway; I'll be out here."

"That's OK. Got a place to get some gas, by the way? Might as well get her all filled up tonight."

"Sure thing. And I'll drive you down to the café to dinner, if you want."

Dinner at the café, with little bits of Louisiana thrown in for flavor. Lyle Adams is a Yankee. Came south to do a little dusting and turned out he liked it and stayed and started his own dusting business. Spraying, nowadays, mostly spraying and seeding. Not a whole lot of dusting still being done. The big modern Ag-Cat is a misty distant offspring of the Parks and her era. A working airplane, with a chemical hopper instead of a front cockpit, all metal and biplane. The Cat looks modern and efficient, and is both. Adams trusts it wholly, loves the machine.

"Great airplane, great airplane. All that wing, she just turns on a dime and gets right back into the field. Course she's not like an old airplane at all. I used to fly a Howard, up in Minnesota. Take hunters and fishermen out to places where no one'd ever been before. Land in the fields . . . I remember one time I took four of these guys way up north . . ."

The hours spin around swiftly, as they always do when new friends meet. At last the café lights go out and we rattle back in the ADAMS FLYING SERVICE pickup truck to the black green grass under the black yellow wing under a shimmering black sky.

"You sure got a lot of stars down here, Lyle."

"Kind of a nice place to live, all right. If you like to farm. If you like to fly airplanes, too. Pretty nice place. You're welcome to sleep at the house, now, like I say. Can't say as I'd make you come, though, night like this. Fact, I should bring my bag out and sleep under that wing with you. Long time since I done any of that. . . ."

The handshake in the dark, the wishes for good sleep, the assurances of meeting when the sun comes up tomorrow, and the pickup is crunching away, dwindling its light, quiet, turning the corner, flickering behind a row of trees, gone.

# 9

Morning. No, not morning even, just a glow in the direction from which we came last night. The sleeping bag is stowed away in the front cockpit, and with it the last bit of warmth in all the state of Louisiana. The air that I breathe steams about me and the rubber of the tall old tires is brittle and hard. My fingers don't work well at pulling the cowling hold-down clips. The gasoline, as I drain a little of it to check for water, is like liquid hydrogen across my hands. Perhaps I should warm the oil. Drain it out and put it in a big can over the fire, the way the barnstormers used to do with their oil on cold nights. Too late now. Pull the drain plug this morning and the oil wouldn't even pour. It would just lie there in the tank and huddle for warmth.

White lights sweep suddenly across the Parks, and rolling truck wheels crunch again on the gravel.

"*Morn*ing!"

"Oh, morning, Lyle. How are you, beside frozen solid?"

"Cold? Man, this is great weather! Little chill makes you feel like workin', of a morning. You 'bout ready for breakfast?"

"Don't think so, this morning. Want to go as far as we can today, use all the daylight. Thanks the same."

"What daylight you talking about? Sun won't be up enough to fly by for another half hour. And you've got to have some breakfast. Hop in, café's just a minute down the road."

I should explain that I don't like breakfasts. I should tell him that the time till sunup should be spent warming the engine. Perhaps the engine won't even start, in the cold, or it might take half an hour to get it to fire.

But the pickup's door is open in the dark, it is clear that everyone in this state expects a person to eat breakfast, and the task of explaining my hurry is much more difficult than stepping into a truck and closing a door. So I'll lose half an hour, trade it for a doughnut and a quick view of a duster pilot's morning.

A Louisiana duster pilot, I discover, knows everyone in town, and everyone in town is at the café before sunup. As we walk heavy-booted into the bright-lit room, setting the brass doorbells jingling, the sheriff and the farmers look around from their coffee to wish a good morning to the president of the Adams Flying Service. And they mean it, for his good mornings, with smooth air and without wind, are theirs, too. In the calm, his ag-planes can work constantly over their fields, seeding and spraying and killing leaf rollers and lygus bugs and darkling ground beetles, animals that once destroyed both fields and farmers. Lyle Adams is an important and respected man in Rayville.

[99]

I collect stares for my strangeness and scarf and heavy flying jacket. Lyle Adams, who lives the same world as I, who worries about engines and flies open-cockpit biplanes every day from the Rayville Airport, collects "Mornin'," and "How're'y'?" and "You workin' the rice today, aren't y', Lyle?" My host is not an aviator in this town, he is a business-man and a farmer, and a little bit of a savior, a protecting god.

I learn, over a black formica tabletop and a cup of hot chocolate, what to expect as I fly west, to the Texas border.

"You want to stay by the road, going out of here. If you go down in the trees a mile off the road, it will be months before they find you. First part of the way, 'round here, is fine . . . you got the fields to land in if you need. But thirty, forty miles out, you better stick by the road.

"Don't know the land much into Texas, but after a while you got fields again, and a little place to come down. Weather's been good the last days, wind picks up toward noon, be a tailwind for you. We might get some thunder-storms the afternoon, but by then you'll be long gone. . . ."

If I ever have need for a detailed knowing of how to fly Louisiana, I can draw on the experience that passed across the tabletop in the café at Rayville. For a moment I am listening to a lonely man, an aviator marooned on an island where no one speaks his language. There is not another person in town who would be happy to know that tailwinds are promised today, or who would be grateful for a warning about trees in the west. My host is practicing a language he doesn't often speak, and it is clear that he enjoys the practice.

"You get a big high-pressure cell sits up over Oklahoma, and the weather's good for days. But with the Gulf down there, we get our share of bad stuff, too. You get so that you know the land pretty well, where the wires are, and that sort of thing, and you can work even when the weather isn't too good. . . ."

By the time the buildings across the street are turning dull red in the dawn, the truck is crunching once again through the gravel, squeaking again to stop by the Parks' bright wingtip.

"Can I give you a hand, here? Help you at all?"

"Sure. You can hop in that cockpit, if you want, Lyle, while I crank the starter. Couple shots of prime, maybe; pump the throttle. She should catch the first time."

The steel handle of the starter handcrank jutting from the cowl is like the steel of an ice-cube tray, cubes installed. I can feel the frost of it through my gloves.

Stiffly, at the very first, t-u-r-n. (Whirring sounds, slowly, within.) And. Turn. And . . . turn; and . . . turn and . . . turn and, turn and turn and turn and turn, turn, turn turn turn turn-turnturnturn . . . pull the crank as the inertia wheel screams and clatters inside, ready to engage and slam its energy into the propeller.

"CLEAR! HIT IT, LYLE!"

One very tiny clink of the *Engage* handle pulled, the falling scream of the starter and one Wright Whirlwind engine blows silence into ten million tiny pieces. The president of Adams Flying Service is smothered and lost for an instant in a cloud of smoke the color of pure blue fire. Another instant, and the smoke is twisting and shredding in the propellerblast, is tumbling back toward the sun glow, through a fence, and gone.

A tiny voice, shouting from the center of a hurricane:

"STARTS RIGHT UP, DON'T SHE?"

"NICE OLD AIRPLANE! LET HER IDLE ABOUT 900 RPM; TAKE HER A WHILE TO GET WARM."

Ten minutes of warming time for the Whirlwind, of cooling time for its pilot. Ten minutes in shouted promises to stop by if I'm ever in the country again, in assurance that I'll be looked up if Lyle Adams makes it out to the West Coast. No goodbyes at all. A fringe benefit of flying, that: a host of friends in odd little places around the world, and the knowing that chances are you'll see them all again, someday.

It was cold enough at ground level; now, at two thousand feet, it is colder than freezing, if that is possible. The highway writhes westward, the trees close back in through Shreveport and across the state line into Texas, almost unseen.

It's like an ice-frozen towel, this wind, pulling and chafing across my face, never stopping. I have to swallow time and again, and it is hard to breathe. The sun crawls up grudgingly, unawake. Even after it is well above the horizon, it refuses to warm the air.

By slipping the leather gloves forward on my fingers, I discover that I can keep them warm for nearly a minute. Stomping up and down on the rudder pedals and turning the big invisible crank does nothing but transform me from cold to cold-and-tired. Below, on the road, no automobiles yet by which to gage my ground speed, though early smoke shows a tailwind. Good, a tailwind is almost worth freezing for, when one sets out to cover as many miles as he can in a day's race.

Even so, I think of landing soon, so that I can stand still, or curl up in a ball and get warm. I wonder if it would be possible to fly an airplane without getting out of one's sleeping bag. Someone should invent a sleeping bag with legs in it, and arms, so that aviators can keep warm when they cross the South. The invention would come a little late, though. Splash it across every magazine and newspaper in the country, put it in every sporting goods store, and even so one probably couldn't make much money on an Aviator's Form Fitting Sleeping Bag. Not too many aviators left around that have a great deal of need for them. Those that do will have to take second-best, rely upon an old-fashioned medium-heat G-type star, and hope that it is quick to rise in the mornings.

I look for a groundspeed indicator, for any wheeled vehicle to move along the road, against which I can compare my speed. No luck. Hey, drivers! Sun's up! Let's get going down there! One single automobile wheeling down the road toward me. He's no help. Three minutes pass. Five, in the coarse hard wind. At last, turning out of a driveway, a green sedan, heading west. A few moments to allow him to reach his cruising speed; should be about sixty-five this morning with the roads clear. And we pass him handily. It is a good tailwind. I wonder if he knows that he is very important to me, whether he knows that there is an old biplane aloft this morning and watching him. Probably doesn't. Probably doesn't even know what a biplane is.

Even freezing, one learns. Something learned about course and speed from someone who is paying attention only to his own course and speed and who doesn't even know I exist. We owe much to green sedans, and the only way that we can pay our debt to them is just to go our way as best we can and be an indicator ourselves without knowing when, for someone we have never seen.

How many times, I ask, grateful now for the first particle of warmth from the east, have I taken freely and used the example that other men have set in their own lives? My whole life is patterned on examples that others have set. Examples to follow, examples to avoid. More than I can count. The ones that stand out, surely I can single them out, the ones that have greatly formed my own thought. Who am I, after all, but a culmination of my time, one meld of every example that has been set and in turn one single example for another to see and judge? I am a little of Patrick Flanagan, a little of Lou Pisane. There is in my hands a little of the skill of flight instructors named Bob Keech and Jamie Forbes and Lieutenant James Rollins. I am part of the skill, too, of Captain Bob Saffell, one of the few survivors of the air-ground war in Korea; of Lieutenant Jim Touchette, who happily fought the whole Air Force when he thought it was being stupid and who died as he turned a flaming F-86 away from an Arizona schoolyard; of Lieutenant Colonel John Makely, a gruff rock of a squadron commander who cared about nothing but the mission of his squadron and the men who flew its airplanes; of Emmett Weber, of Don Slack, of Ed Carpinello, of Don McGinley, of Lee Morton, of Keith Ulshafer, of Jim Roudabush, of Les Hench, of Dick Travas, of Ed Fitzgerald. So many names, so many pilots, and a little bit of each one of them is in me at the moment I fly an old biplane through a blue-cold Louisiana dawn.

Without bending a bit of effort, I can open my eyes to the great crowd of pilots who are flying this airplane. There's Bo Beaven, looking across at me and nodding coolly. Hank Whipple, who barrel-rolled a cargo transport and taught me how to land in pastures and on beaches and tried so hard to teach me to think far ahead of the airplane and of those who would restrict flight through their own fears and through meaningless regulation. Christy Cagle, who set an example about enjoying old airplanes, who would rather sleep under the wing of his biplane than in any bed.

In the crowd are other teachers, too. Look there, the shining silver Luscombe that first took me away from the jealous ground. A big round-engined T-28 that itself called the crash trucks by trailing a stream of black smoke from its damaged engine, at a time when I was too new to flying to know even that there was something wrong. A Lockheed T-33, the first jet airplane I ever flew, that taught me that an airplane can be flown by holding the control stick in thumb and forefinger and *thinking* climbs and dives and turns. There's a beauty-queen F-86F to show me how strongly a pilot can become enchanted and in love with his airplane. A little dragonfly of a helicopter, to point the fun of standing still in the air. An ice-blue Schweizer 1-26 sailplane, telling of the invisible things that can keep a pilot drifting on the wind for hours without need of an engine. The good old rocksolid F-84F, covering my mistakes and telling me many things during a night flight over France. A Cessna 310, saying that an airplane can get so luxurious that the pilot is hardly aware it has a personality at all. A Republic Seabee, saying there's no fun quite like turning from a speedboat into an airplane and back, feeling clear water splash and sparkle along the hull. A 1928 Brunner-Winkle Bird biplane, asking me to taste the fun of flying with a pilot who has found a forgotten airplane, spent years rebuilding it and who at last turns it free once again in the air. A Fairchild 24, that in several hundred hours of exploring the sky brought me the sudden revelation that the sky is a real, true, tangible, touchable place. A C-119 troop carrier, much maligned, that taught me not to believe what I hear about "bad airplanes" until I have a chance to see for myself, and that there can be a good feeling in throwing the green-light *Jump* signal and dropping a stick of paratroopers where they want to go. And today, an old biplane, trying to cross the country.

Fast or slow, quiet or deafening, pulling contrails at forty thousand feet or whishing wheels through the grasstops, in barest simplicity or most opulent luxury, they are all there, teaching and having taught. They all are a part of the pilot and he is a part of them. The chipped paint of a control

[105]

console, the rudder pedals worn smooth during twenty years of turns, the control stick grips from which the little knurl diamonds have been rubbed away: these are the marks of a man upon his airplane. The marks of an airplane upon the man are seen only in his thought, and in the things that he has learned and come to believe.

Most pilots I have known are not what they have seemed. They are two very separate people within the same body. Pick out a name . . . and here's Keith Ulshafer, the perfect example. Here's a man you'd never expect to see in a fighter squadron. When Keith Ulshafer said a word, it was a major occasion. Keith had no need to impress anybody; if you were to step in front of him and say, "You're a crummy pilot, Keith," he'd smile and he'd say, "Probably am." It was impossible to make him angry. He couldn't be hurried. He approached flying as though it were a problem in integral calculus. Although he had calculated his takeoff roll hundreds of times, and when any other pilot would look outside and feel the wind and temperature and guess the takeoff distance within fifty feet, Keith would figure it out with the planning charts before every flight and write it in carefully-penciled figures at the bottom of a form that was rarely read. Neat, precise, meticulous. For Keith to hurry or to guess an airspeed or a fuel-consumption figure would have been for a chief accountant to step into the ring with the Masked Phantom. It was almost a joke to sit in a preflight briefing with him and listen to the flight leader outline the details of an air combat mission. Not a word from Keith as the wild vocabulary of the mission to come flew about his ears, as if he were a correspondent for a technical journal that happened to be sitting in the wrong chair when the briefing began. You'd never know that he was listening at all until the end of the briefing, when he might softly say, "You mean two-fifty-*six* point four megacycles for channel twelve, don't you?" and the flight leader would stand corrected. More often Keith wouldn't say a word when the briefing was done. He'd amble to his locker, zip his G-suit slowly about his legs, shrug into his flight jacket, emblazoned by regulation with lightnings and swords and fierce words that are supposed to typify fighter pilots. Then, carrying his parachute as something a little bit distasteful, he'd stroll to his airplane.

Even the boom of his starter firing wasn't as sudden as those of other airplanes, and his engine wasn't as loud.

Keith flew by the book. In formation, his airplane did not bounce or rock from side to side. It was as solid as if it had been bolted to the wing of the lead airplane. Then the mission, the air combat, would begin. And then, of course, look out.

Flying straight up, flying straight down, rolling streaking twisting flashing through the sky whirled the airplane that you would have sworn had Keith Ulshafer aboard when it left the ground. It was as though Keith had hopped quickly out before takeoff and some wild stranger had gotten in. You felt like pressing the microphone button and asking, "You all right, Keith?"

Keith was all right, and with luck and with attention and with very great skill you might be able to dodge the incredible monster at the controls of his airplane. On other missions of combat, it was always there. Here comes Keith, blazing down on the strafing target, the ground disintegrating in front of him; here he is closing on the Dart, towed for target practice, and blowing the silver thing out of the sky; down he drops on the rocket target and puts four rockets in a fifteen-foot circle. On close air support missions in the war games, Keith comes blasting in just high enough to clear the tanks' whip antenna, pulling up after the last pass in a flawless set of matched aileron rolls, disappearing into the sun. In the landing pattern he flies close and tight to the runway, touching his wheels precisely on the line painted as a touchdown target. Then, while the armorers de-arm the guns, the wildman jumps down from the cockpit, runs into the woods, and the other Keith Ulshafer, the technical-journal correspondent, strolls back in and he takes off his jacket and he unzips his G-suit.

There is, I am learning, sleeping within us all, a person who lives only for times of instant decision and quick-blurring action. I saw him a year ago in Keith's wildman, I met him yesterday as a gambler in my biplane. In all of us this person sleeps, in the most unlikely person that logic could pick.

Over Texas, the pine trees are falling back and the plains begin to open ahead. The sun at last is warm in the air and the tailwind holds good; even the fastest automobiles are whisking backward beneath the wings.

I can see the tailwind, when I close my eyes, and I can see the biplane, a tiny dot borne along in it. The tailwind is only one eddy in a huge whirlpool of moving air, a whirlpool turning clockwise about a great center of high pressure somewhere to the north. An airplane flying at this moment in precisely the same direction as I, but north of that center, would be struggling through headwinds. My tailwind cannot hold, of course. I am flying away from the center, and even though I move only a little over one hundred miles per hour I will be able to see the winds begin to change about me before too long. Already, in two hours of flying, the wind has changed from a direct tailwind to a tailwind quartering slightly from the south. In another few hours it will be a crosswind from the south, drifting me to the right of course, and I shall have to fly as low as possible to avoid its ill effects.

Beware the winds that drift you to the right, I have learned. The maxim: "Drift Right into Danger." To drift to the right is to leave the zone of high pressure and good weather and to enter the frowning centers of low pressure and lowering clouds and visibility diminishing down to a mist in the sky. If I turned now just a little to the right, to keep the wind directly on my tail, I could begin a circle that would keep me always in clear weather; I would fly a circle with the whirlpool, about the high. But I would end where I began. To make progress along a course, I must expect a storm or two. But I am grateful for the good already received, the days of pure weather that have attended us. And still it holds; as far as I can see, there is no sign of lowering weather ahead.

Before me on the plain, the first smudge of a city rising. Dallas. Or more properly, Dallas/Fort Worth. Gradually it lifts and looms clearer, a giant sprawled in the sunlight. I shift course to the south, to avoid flying over the city. It should look like any other city from the air, but it does not. I cannot look at Dallas objectively. There has been a furious battle raging over airports in Dallas/Fort Worth. Each claims to have the airport most suited to the needs of both cities, and at last the government had to step in and mediate the case. Much name calling going on down there, and bad feeling among those who used to fly and are now the operators of Large Steel Desks with "Airport Official" written in nameplates.

Beyond that, the city is a big depressing place, and there is even a sad tone in the sound of the engine, a going-lower sound from the cylinders. This is the city where the President was shot. I am glad that I do not have to land.

The mood of the countryside brightens a bit when the city has fallen out of sight behind, and I find U.S. Highway 80, which will be my primary navigation aid for the next thousand miles. Somewhere soon I should think about landing.

Western Hills, it says on the map, and I fly one circle about a little town and its airport. It is 8:30 in the morning, but there is not a sign of life on the field. The hangars are closed, the parking lot is empty. I will surely have to wait for fuel. I have made good time in the wind and down the road will be another airport at which someone is stirring. Besides, every mile behind is one less mile ahead. Considering this rather basic maxim of the traveler in the open cockpit, I settle down once again with the W of the magnetic compass bobbling under the reference line. By now the wind is a full crosswind and there is nothing to be gained by remaining at altitude. Forward on the stick, then, and down we come into the layer of the sky where the wind is slowed by its contact with the ground. We level fifty feet in the air above the deserted highway and rise and fall with the contour of the low hills.

Here and there an automobile on the road, and I get to know each one well, for I do not pass them so quickly now. A station wagon built sometime way ahead in the years to come, with children who haven't yet been born crowding the rear windows. I wave to them, across time and across five hundred feet of Texas air, and receive in return a little forest of waving hands. It is comforting to see other people moving through this space, and I cannot help but wonder what the others think as they look back into 1929. Does it remind them? Do they remember the days when they crossed this very road (it was a dirt road then) and along about there in the sky was an airplane just like that one that is there now? And it pulled slowly ahead and it vanished gradually to the left of the road, just as that one is vanishing?

I fly the up-sun side of the road from habit, and I wonder if that was a habit in the first days of flight. Probably not. Fly up-sun and they can't read your number. A defensive sort of habit, that. But I think it has saved me trouble now and then.

There are not many people who know that it is perfectly permissible for an airplane to fly at less-than-treetop height in uninhabited land. If someone were not feeling happy about old airplanes, they could catch my big registration number and cause me to have to prove my innocence. The regulations say only that I must fly five hundred feet from any person on the ground; whether the five hundred feet is over or to one side of him makes no difference. Now, avoiding the wind and with plenty of smooth places to land, I choose to fly five hundred feet to one side of. The up-sun side.

When the road is clear, I fly over till my wheels straddle the centerline and I sit up tall in the seat and crane over the windscreen and over the long nose and just enjoy flying low. The telephone poles whisk by, and by resting one elbow on the rim of the cockpit I feel again almost as if I am driving an automobile. With the one fine difference of being able to touch back on my steering control and go roaring straight up into the sky.

I have a friend who is a race-car driver and he says racing is the greatest fun in the world. For him; he keeps forgetting to say, for him. For anyone else—well, for me—it is a frightening sort of fun. As in so many pursuits that are pinned to the ground, there is no margin, no time for thinking of other things. He must stay precisely upon that narrow ribbon of asphalt, and if anything looms ahead or even if the ribbon is not properly banked, the driver is in trouble. He has to think hard about driving every second that he holds that accelerator down. The sky, on the other hand, and very happily, is for dreamers, because there is so much margin, so much freedom. In an old airplane the takeoff and the landing are a bit critical, but the flying itself is the simplest, most controllable way to travel since . . . since nothing at all. Something in the way ahead? Climb over it. Turn around it. Fly underneath it. Circle for a while and think about it. None of these can the race driver do. He can only try to stop. With his margin, the airplane pilot can sit back in his cockpit and relax. He can spend long minutes looking behind his airplane, or above it or below it. Looking ahead is a sort of formality that has carried over from habits learned on the ground. He can do anything he wants to do with the ground; tilt it, twist it, put it over his head or directly behind his tail. And he can let it just wander its sleepy way below and look down at it through slitted eyes and make it go all misty and unreal.

The signs and the warnings and the agencies of flight remind solemnly that one should never let his attention shift from the urgent task of flying his airplane, that to let the mind drift for a second is disaster. But, after one has been flying for a very short while, it becomes clear that the agencies take themselves far too seriously. As a student pilot learns early in his first lesson, an airplane will fly itself better than he can fly it. An airplane does not demand the constant concentrated thought to stay in the air that the race car demands to stay on its narrow road. Following only the basic caution of not flying into a tree or the side of a mountain, a pilot finds the sky a perfect place to go and not-think.

Now, driving a foot above Highway 80 in my airplane, I must be a little more cautious than in those hours when there are five hundred or a thousand feet between my wheels and the earth. Now I can be the race driver, but without the penalty that plagues him. If I miss the turn, I can go right on over the guard rail, on over the rocks and boulders and the trees, and not feel the slightest tremor in my machine.

Over the rise of a hill ahead, unexpectedly, a car driving toward me. Back hard on the stick, and a turn into the sun, to gain that five hundred feet. I can't help but smile within myself. What would that feel like for me, to be driving over a little rise of ground along an ordinary road way out in nowhere and suddenly be confronted with an airplane headed directly at my windshield? That's not a very kind thing for an airplane pilot to do to people, despite the legality of it, and I should peek over the hills before I allow the biplane to frighten some poor driver who would rather be alone with his even-chuffing train of thought.

So we go our way, peeking over the hills first, then pressing

ourselves tightly to the road, rolling our wheels once or twice on either side of the white line without really meaning to.

A bit of a start as I glance at my watch, for I have been flying for over four hours and am far ahead of my estimate for this hour. Ahead, the town of Ranger, Texas, listed on the map as home to an airport. I climb to see better, and find the water tower, the crossing of another highway, a building being built. And an airport. It is a big airport for such a small town, three dirt runways crossed on the ground and a pair of hangars. Circle once, check the windsock and, with a silent

word of thanks to the man who decided to have more than one runway available for landing, turn into the wind and settle to the dirt.

It is not even lunchtime and I have covered five hundred miles from Louisiana. That seems like so much, and I am proud, but away in the future/past I have flown airplanes that covered that distance in less than an hour, and one that could cover it in twenty minutes. There should be something meaningful in the contrast, in the shifting spectrums of times and airplanes, but now I am tired from four hours of sitting on a stone-hard parachute, and at the moment the meanings come second to the luxury of standing up and taking a step along an unmoving ground. The flight is going like a welcome routine, everything according to plan and as I would have it. And at the moment, at Ranger, Texas, as I wipe the oil from the windscreens and from the cowl, I do not think of the plan or of the future.

# 1 0

"SORRY, MISTER. I can't swing that prop for you. Can't turn the crank, either. Insurance. My insurance wouldn't cover me if I got hurt."

Strange strange strange, and I'm furious as I storm from the cockpit where I have been ready for engine start. Come all this way having too many willing helpers to tend the biplane and now, in a hurry to be gone, I have to get out here in the ninety-degree sun in a fur-lined jacket and I have to crank the airplane by myself, while the attendant stands back and watches. Anger converts easily into energy, and by the time the inertia flywheel is screaming I am too tired to bother with the fears of the attendant. Pull the starter engage handle, let the engine roar into life and shake a blanket of dry dust behind, taxi to face the wind, run the engine and let go the brakes. A glance at my watch as the wheels lift from the ground and I begin to tick away another four hours, second by second. I settle down upon my friend the highway and it is as if I had not landed at all, as if I have been sitting constantly behind this propeller from sunrise, and from the night before that and from the day that led into the night. It will be good to get to California and home.

The crosswind has turned now to become a strong breeze, pushing me hard to the right, so that I must fly angled to the highway, fighting the wind with the bright blade of my propeller.

Fighting the wind with the blade. That is sort of poetic. But, when one is pressed shoulder to shoulder with the roiling forces that travel the sky, one needs every weapon he can get. A propeller is one of the pilot's weapons, for as long as it turns he is not really thrown on his own. As long as it turns it is not just a man against the crosswind or the headwinds or the ice over sea, but a man and his airplane, working and fighting together. One doesn't feel quite so lonely. Still, the propeller is not a friend without weakness, and to know the weakness and to supply the need of the weapon in those times is a wise practice. A propeller can be bravely turning full revolutions, as fast as it can turn, and if the airplane flies into a mass of air that is falling faster than the airplane can climb, it is all to no avail and the weapon and the pilot slide toward the earth. But the simple forethought of seeing the weakness and supplying it, of knowing that one can escape downdraft, and turn a mile away to a place where the air is rising, fills the coffers with altitude. So, before the weapon is even un-sheathed for battle, before it is needed or the battle has been joined, the man in the airplane can supply the needs of his weapon. Enter this valley on the right side or the left? On one side will be a constant fight, a furious running duel with the wind and the mountain. On the other side, perhaps less than a mile distant, a smooth flight, that needs even less power than normal to maintain altitude. So, as he learns, the pilot begins to think not of left side or right, but upwind side or downwind. At first the student pilot would seek to disregard the wind, to cast it from his thought, for he has too many problems already to concern him, and give him one good reason why he should bother with something he can't even see. The answer, the student learns, is simply to be able to see the wind. The wind is a giant ocean of air surging along the rocky floor of the earth. Where ocean waves would tumble green and rushing down the side of the mountain, look for the wind to do the same. Where ocean would smash against the base of a cliff and shoot straight up, see there, on a day when the wind is strong, a power that will take an airplane by the wings and throw it headlong into the sky. Fly always the upwind side of the mountains and hills and you can fly easily, in the conscious power of one who knows that he needn't even loose his weapon to win a battle or to avoid it.

Where there are no mountains, the pilot who sees the sky sees tall columns of warm blue air rising from heated spots on the ground. Pause for a moment in one of the columns, circling, and the airplane climbs in spite of itself, carried aloft on an elevator denied to those who believe only what they can surely see. The man who flies an airplane, then, to be the best possible pilot, must be a believer in the unseen.

One can get along in the air for a long time without having to believe, for usually the only consequence of unbelieving is a little more strain on the engine, a little more wear on the propeller. But if one flies long enough and far enough there will come the day when the difference between believing and not believing is the difference between winning or losing the whole game of problem solving.

Ahead, the sky goes brown in dust thrown by the wind. Dust that is Texas airborne, and one of the reasons behind the poignant names of Texas towns along my course: Gladewater, Clearwater, Sweetwater, Mineral Wells, Big Spring. A land centered about water, and where the water is scarce in the ground it is made plentiful in thought and in the names of cities.

I look up and see that the dust tops out way over my head . . . six thousand, maybe eight thousand feet. It would be useless to try to climb over it; the winds aloft would be even more on my nose and I would find the cars passing me. As it is, I can stay with the faster autos, just barely hold my own. That is a disconcerting feeling. There is a blue station wagon on the highway, humming along. It falls behind me a little when it has to climb a hill, it catches up and moves on ahead when the hill is in its favor. We have been together for minutes, so long that the passengers no longer bother to look out the window at the biplane flying not far away. The woman is reading a newspaper. I wonder if she knows that I'm looking over her shoulder. Of course not. You wouldn't expect the pilot of an *airplane* to be aware of a car on the road, let alone of the people in the car.

The great wide flat land is all about, as far as I can see. There is room to put ten thousand biplanes into safe harbor. If the dust ahead gets so thick that I cannot see, it will be simple to turn and face the wind and land on any short stretch of clear soil. The stronger the wind, the shorter the space that the biplane will use for a safe landing. If the wind reaches fifty-five miles per hour, I'll be able to land without even rolling the wheels. I could hover for an hour above my landing spot if I wished, and alight as gently as hummingbird upon jasmine branch. Still, the wind across the ground looks vicious, whipping long lashes of sand across the highway, making the dry trees bow and flutter to the force of its will.

We press ahead and I find myself wondering what comes next, from out of the murk, wondering whether the dust and the wind are all that are lying behind the portent of this ominous right drift. Somehow, there is that part of my thought that will be disappointed if there is not something more carnivorous than this waiting to battle.

The little towns of the brown plain slowly appear and slowly vanish behind as the wind shifts to blow more directly against the front of the biplane. Of course, I remind myself, the wind is not blowing on the airplane at all; the only wind that I feel is the wind that the airplane makes in its passage through the air and the blast of the propeller at work. We are like a goldfish in a deep river of air, swimming through the air and at the same time being carried along in its bosom. The classic illustration for the young in flight is, "If you are aloft in a balloon in a hurricane, you could light a candle in the open air and the flame wouldn't even flicker. You're moving just as fast as the wind, my friend, just like a goldfish in a river."

I doubt that the candle/hurricane theory has ever been tested, but it all seems very logical and the goldfish must know that it is true. Still, it is difficult to accept this totally from the windy, gritty cockpit of an airplane over a long and lonely highway. Perhaps if I had a candle . . .

If I had a candle, I would still need the balloon. Settle down, pilot, and think about your flying. If the visibility gets very much worse, you know, you are going to have to land.

One solitary automobile on the highway passes me handily and I must draw my comfort from the fact that it is a new and luxurious machine. He could probably go one hundred miles per hour if he wanted to. In the tiny towns, the people have left the outdoors to the wind, and for the long minutes that the collection of houses drift beneath me they bring rippling reflections of the little villages along the roads of France. Deserted. Utterly deserted. Shutters closed, even in the center of the day. I never did discover where French villagers live, and left Europe as mystified as the other squadron pilots as to what the villages and the houses were for.

Vaguely through the sand comes a longer line of gasoline stations clinging to the highway. There is a city coming, and I look to the map on my knee. City city city, let's see. City should be . . . Big Spring. A strange name, at this moment. North of the city there will be an airport and I should think about landing. No, I won't land. There are two hours left in the tank, and I might fly out of the worst of the dust if I continue. Climb to cross the city, although I'm certain that no one hears the sound of five cylinders over the howl of the wind. Still, in a few things, conforming to regulation becomes a habit. Seven minutes to cross the city. I am certainly not moving very quickly. But if I stick to my task the wind should shift to become a right crosswind, drifting me to the left and portending good things to come.

A long wait. The parachute turns again to stone beneath me, incapable of being the cushion it was designed to be. A gradual Midland floats past below. An equally gradual Odessa, with tall buildings reaching up out of the depths of the ground and making me feel a little giddy to look down the lengths of them. Like many pilots, I would rather fly to fifty thousand feet in an airplane than look over the edge of a two-story building. A few people in the streets of Odessa, clothes flapping. And ahead; isn't the sky growing a little brighter? I squint my eyes behind the goggles and maybe, just maybe, the sky is clearer to the west. And the expectant in me goes dead. This is all there will be. A brief dust storm, not even wild in its briefness, and the adversary is defeated. I circle in to land at Monahans and need less than one hundred feet of runway to roll to a stop. What a safe feeling. I can practically fly the airplane after it is on the ground, in the wind alone.

Once facing away from the wind, though, one must be very careful on the ground. An airplane is not built to move slowly along the ground, and unless it moves cautiously and uses its flight controls carefully, a strong wind can pick it up and casually, uncaringly, throw it on its back. It can take many insults from the sun and the weather as it stands on the ground, but one of the two things it cannot take is a very strong wind. The other, of course, is hail.

Easy easy now to the gas pump. Swing into the wind. Let the gritty engine die. It is a shame that there will be no more dragons to attack on this trip. Ahead can only be better weather and later even a tailwind once more. Those first pilots didn't have such a very difficult time of it, after all. Only a little part of Texas to cross, part of New Mexico and Arizona, and we are home. Almost an uneventful flight. If I hurry, I can be home tomorrow night.

So thinking, I put the hose to the gas tank and watch the scarlet fuel pour into the blackness.

# 1 1

THE SKY IS ALMOST CLEAR when we once again trade land underwheel for sky underwing and turn to follow our faithful navigation highway, which lies like a cracked arrow pointing toward El Paso. Tonight at El Paso, or if I'm lucky, at Deming, New Mexico. We fly low once again with the sky burnt umber in the dust at our back and the sun turning quietly to shine in our eyes. We fly through a tall invisible gate, into the desert. The desert is very suddenly there and looks at us with a perfectly blank expression; no smiles, no frowns. The desert simply is there, and it waits.

Dimly ahead, hazy blue outlines, mountains. They are mountains still of fantasy, faint and softly shimmering. There are three of them, to the left, to the right, and one, with impossibly steep sides, barely to the right of course. The sleeping thirster for adventure wakes, saying, Perhaps a battle? What comes ahead? What do you see out there? A chance to wrestle against great odds? But I put him once again murmuring to sleep with the assurance that there are no windmills ahead, no dragons to slay.

For long minutes as I fly, I relax in the sun and the wind, the biplane needing only a gentle touch to follow its white-line compass down the road to the horizon. The road turns imperceptibly to the left and the airplane turns to follow. The sun and the wind are soft and warm and there is little to do but wait for this flight to reach El Paso, as though I had bought my airline ticket in Monahans and now it is up to the captain to bring me to destination.

I can never help thinking, as I cross the deserts, of those who looked through this air a hundred years ago, when the sun was a fireball in the sky and the wind was a jagged knife along the ground. What brave people. Or did they leave their homes for the West not out of bravery but out of just not knowing what lay ahead along this path? I look for wagon tracks and find none. There is only the highway, the Johnny-come-lately highway, and this white line, angling south of west.

They deserve a lot of respect. Months to cross a continent, that even an old biplane can cross in a mere week. A cliché, that, and easily said mockingly. But it is hard, over this land, not to think of those people. Imagine that, *people* down there on the surface, in the sun, driving oxen! If the sameness and the mile-on-mile exist for a biplane that covers seventy miles in a single hour, how much more it must have existed for them during those months.

Looking up from the gunbarrel road to the horizon, a little shock of ice, and within me the adventurer jerks bolt upright. The three mountains are there ahead, and clearer. But the mountain in the center, with the impossibly steep sides, has moved to stand squarely across my path. From the top of it drifts a short anvil of white. And now beneath it I can see a black column of angled rain. I'm not alone out here after all; the tall white thunderstorm ahead is an absorbing, hypnotic personality in the sky.

Easily avoided. Plenty of room to give it a wide berth; I'll just swing around to the right. . . . FIGHT IT! It is the adventurer, wide awake now and looking for bright quick things to happen. FIGHT IT, BOY! YOU'RE NOT SOME SHRINKING FEARFUL NAMBY-PAMBY, ARE YOU? YOU GOT ANY COURAGE AT ALL YOU'LL FLY THROUGH THAT THING! THAT'S EXCITEMENT OVER THERE, THAT'S SOMETHING THAT NEEDS TO BE CONQUERED!

Oh, go back to bed. I'd be out of my mind to fly through that storm. At the very least I'd get soaking wet, and at worst the thing would tear the biplane to shreds.

The cloud looms over me now and I can see the anvil of it towering way up high over the top wing of the biplane. I have to tilt my head back to see the end of it in the sky. We begin a turn to the right.

OK. Fine. Turn away. You're afraid of it. That's fine, there's nothing wrong with being afraid of a thunderstorm. Of course the rain beneath it is not a tenth as bad as flying through the center, and I'm not asking you to fly through the center, just the rain. A very mild little adventure. Look, you can almost see through the rain to the other side of the storm, where it's clear again. Go ahead. Turn away. But just you don't talk to me about courage any more. Mister, if you don't fly through this one little patch of rain, you don't have the faintest idea of what courage is. Nothing wrong with that, nothing wrong with being afraid and being a coward, but, son-of-a-gun, you better not let me catch you thinking about bravery any more.

It is childish, of course. Not the courageous, but the foolhardy would fly under a storm when avoiding it is a matter only of a shallow turn to the right. Ridiculous. If I believe in caution and prudent action, I will stand up for it and prudently fly around the storm.

The biplane swings to the left and points its nose into the black rain.

It certainly *looks* frightening, close up. But it is just rain, after all, and maybe a tiny bit of turbulence. The top of the cloud is out of sight now, over my head. I tighten the safety belt.

The engine doesn't care. The engine doesn't care if we fly through a tornado. The five cylinders roar on above a wet road, dull under the black base of the cloud.

A light tap of turbulence, just a little thud, and the forward windscreen sprays back the first drops of rain. Here we go. COME ON STORM! YOU THINK YOU'RE BIG ENOUGH TO STOP AN AIRPLANE? THINK YOU'RE BIG ENOUGH TO KEEP ME FROM FLYING RIGHT ON THROUGH?

An instant answer. The world goes grey in a hard sheet of rain, a smashing solid rain much more dense than it had seemed. Even above the roar of the engine and the wind I can hear the rain thundering on the cloth of the wings. Hang on, son.

A thousand feet up in the rain, and abruptly, without warning, the engine stops.

Good God.

Hard turn to the right, looking for a narrow strip to land. You idiot. Wouldn't fly around the thing, would you? Maybe we can land on the highway no the highway is crosswind and we've got to get out of this rain. A few places to land, but they'd be the end of the airplane. Mounds of sand, with tough sage holding them together. What a stupid thing to do. Fly under a thunderstorm.

We float out from under the cloud, and the torrent instantly stops. One beat from the engine, one cylinder firing. Pump the throttle, the primer, if you only would have gone around the rain, throw the magneto switch from *Both* to *Right*, there is the survival kit in the back and the jug of water. Some more cylinders fight into life, but it is an uneven fight; they fire once, miss three times, fire once again. The magnetos. The magnetos must have gotten wet. Of course. Now all they have to do is dry out before we touch the ground. Come along, little magnetos.

Five hundred feet now, and turning toward a clear lane in the sand. If it goes well, I won't hurt the airplane. If everything goes just right. Feel that sun, magnetos. No more storms for you today. A few more cylinders fire, and more often. Switch from right mag to left, and the firing fades completely. Quickly back to right and the propeller blurs faster, and for seconds at a time the engine runs normally. Sounds like those old rotary engines, cutting on and off. And there it is. Still missing every once in a while, but firing enough to keep the biplane in the air. We circle the landing place, three hundred feet above it. Retrieve the map from where it has fallen. Forty miles to the next airport, next airport is Fabens, Texas. Here's a problem for you. Leave a place where I might be able to make a safe landing, or push on across forty miles of desert and hope that the engine will keep running? If I land now and everything goes right, I can let the magnetos dry, take off once again and be sure of reaching El Paso.

And another interesting thing. When the engine stopped, I was not frightened. It was clear that I would have to make a landing; there was no choice. Land. Period. No discussions, no fear.

But now there is time to be concerned. It is not the forced landing that concerns a pilot, but the uncertainty of just when it will come. I can expect the engine to stop at any time; I should not be surprised if it does. I would almost be glad if the engine had not started again; I would be left with no choice but to land, and life would be much simpler. The thing to do now is to get some altitude, staying all the while over the one good strip in the desert. Then I shall set out for Fabens, staying always within gliding distance of a good clear spot. The dumb people who fly under storms.

I discover as the plan turns from thought into action and as the biplane slowly fights for altitude over the desert, engine roaring five seconds, silent for a half-second, roaring six seconds more, that ahead are coming the most difficult forty miles of my journey. There is a definite procedure laid down for pilots to follow if the engine stops, and no fear attendant. But if it doesn't quite stop, what then? I'll have to consider this tonight over a bowl of soup and a glass of ice water.

The biplane flies more slowly than normal, despite the full-open throttle. Pull the throttle back and the engine dies. Switch magnetos and it dies. Under a very special set of conditions it will just barely keep running. We'll give her a try. When she stops, we'll be confident and fearless again. I don't care if I smash her to a splinter heap, I know I'll walk away all right. And other soothing statements.

Skirting the right side of the storm, hardly aware that it exists, I help the little biplane through the sky. Any time I want to frighten myself, I have only to switch from the right mag to the left and listen to the silence. The adventurer is wide awake still, and urges me to overcome the fear in the switch. For his sake, to prove to myself that I am not afraid of listening to the quiet when all about the land below is desert, I switch it. But it is no use. It scares me. Yet if by itself the engine stopped and wouldn't run again, I know that there wouldn't be the slightest fear. Interesting. Lots of little mental relays and shuttle switches working overtime on this leg. From field, to field, to field, to field I travel, engine smoothing for a while, then cutting out again. I have in my mind a picture of the magnetos, the two of them beneath the engine cowling. It is dark in there, with oil mist swirling, but I can see the water in the seams of the magneto housings, and every once in a while another drop splashes down upon them.

I find the road on the other side of the storm and from it gain some measure of comfort. At least now I can land on the road and be near some kind of occasional rolling humanity. I wonder if motorists know how important they are to aviators. They are a source of glee when the tailwinds are there and the airplane passes the automobiles quickly. Glee, too, when the traffic is heavy on the road and a pilot can pass ten cars a second. A reassurance in the desolate lands, bringing their sign of life into view. And a last-ditch help, when glee is gone and one must land on a highway and ask aid.

Over the nose of the biplane, to the right of the road, a search answered. First ahead, then not quite within gliding distance and therefore uncomfortably distant, and at last I have captured Fabens and I don't care if the engine stops or not. I take a sheer cool drink of relief. The wind is heading directly down the dirt strip; blessing on blessing! Throttle back, a gliding turn, steeply, to lose altitude. Imagine that. Too much altitude. I feel like a rich man lighting bonfires with hundred-dollar bills. Level above the dirt, an easing of the stick and we are down again, and stopped. Hurray! Land again beneath me, solid and smooth, and a gas pump! A Coca-Cola machine!

Fabens, Texas, I shall never forget you.

# 12

There is a restaurant in Fabens, part of the motel on U.S. Highway 80. Like every other café and restaurant across the country, in the hour before sunrise, it is a very uncomfortable place for criminals. In Rayville it was the sheriff at breakfast, at Fabens it is the highway patrol. Two beaconed squad cars are parked in the gravel outside and four black-uniformed, six-gunned officers take their coffee at the counter, talking about a murderer caught the night before in El Paso.

I feel guilty as they talk, and glad that they aren't still looking for murderers. I am a suspicious-looking character, sitting alone at the far end of the counter, furtively consuming a doughnut. My flight suit is smeared with rocker-box grease, ingrained with Midland-Odessa sand. My boots are white in runway dust, and I am suddenly aware that the survival knife sewn on my right boot could be a very sinister thing, a concealed weapon. I cross my left boot over the right one, feeling more and more the wary fugitive.

"You want a ride out to the airport, mister?"

I hope the sudden startled clatter of my hot chocolate cup doesn't mark me a murderer.

"You're the fellow with the biplane out there, aren't you?"

"How would you know that?"

"Saw you come in last night. I do a little flying out there myself—Cessna 150."

I forget about my concealed weapon, accept a ride, and the talk changes from murderers to the good old days of flying.

At dawn the magnetos are dry. During the engine runup before takeoff, they don't miss a beat. That was my problem. There can be no other explanation. The magnetos were wet, and as long as I keep them dry I shall have no more difficulties with engines.

So, before the sun is quite up, a single biplane leaves the ground at Fabens, Texas, and turns to follow a highway leading west. It takes a while to settle down again. It was from this cockpit that I saw the unpleasant difficulties of yesterday, and it will be a minute or two before confidence returns that the difficulties are truly gone. Switch the mag selector from *Right* to *Left* and I cannot hear the slightest change in the sound of the engine. I could not ask for a better ignition system. But it is always good practice to keep a landing place in sight.

El Paso, with its very own mountain, in the first light of the sun. I have watched the sun on this mountain before, but I think now of the times quickly, without searching for meaning. I just know that I have been here before, but now I am in a hurry to leave El Paso, a checkpoint only, a dwindling crosshatch behind me.

The road is gone, too, and for the next eighty miles the navigation is the traditional kind: railroad track, and is this ever a *desert!* Visibility must be a hundred miles and it's like looking through a microscope at a sheet of grey newsprint: clumps of desert sage on mounds of sand, each clump precisely eight feet from its neighbors on all sides. Any one clump could be the center of the desert and the rest stretch perfect and absolutely constant to the end of the earth. Even the map gives up here and sighs. The black line of the railroad track races inch on inch through the tiny faceless dots that mean there's nothing out here at all.

Stop now, engine, and we'll discover how long we have to wait for a train to cross these tracks. I dare not fly low. First, to give a wider choice of landing places. Second, because I am afraid that I will see rust upon the tracks.

Right magneto. Fine. Left magneto . . . wasn't that the tiniest missing of a beat, there? It couldn't have been, now quick, switch back to *Both*. Oh, it's whistling-up-courage time. There was the smallest choke then, I'm sure. Automatic Rough, boy, just like the missed beats you hear in any engine as soon as it is over water and out of gliding distance from land. Yesyes that's it, good ol' Automatic Rough, the practical joker, and it won't be necessary to check the mags again.

Listening very closely, I can hear the uneven beat of the engine. The only unanswered question is whether the uneven beat is normal or not, for I have never listened so closely to this engine before. I think that I could listen as closely to a sewing machine and hear the stitches missed. As the mechanics say, you can't fix anything till you see something wrong; I'll just have to wait till the missing gets worse.

Uncomfortable miles of desert pass below. Certainly makes a difference when one suddenly has no trust in an engine. I can't help but think that the less I trust the engine, the less worthy of trust it will be, and my little sewing machine will collapse completely.

There you go, engine; I trust the heck out of you. Run on and on, you little devil; bet I couldn't stop you if I tried, you run so well. Remember your brother engines who set the endurance records and pulled the Spirit of St. Louis from Roosevelt Field to Le Bourget. They wouldn't be at all happy to hear that you considered stopping over the desert, would they? Now, you've got plenty of fuel and there's plenty of oil for you, warm and clean, it is a fine dry morning. Wonderful for flying, don't you think? Yes, it certainly is a fine dry morning.

I am in a hurry, full in a hurry. I do not care now whether I learn or not, the only thing that matters is that this engine keeps running and that we make it quickly to California. Learning is a misty little will-o'-the-wisp that is gone as soon as one blinks one's eyes and allows thought of something else. When I hurry, the airplane goes dead and quiet beneath me, and I grow tired, and I fly a machine in the air and I learn nothing.

Coming in from the horizon is the first curve in the track and around that curve, Deming, New Mexico. We'll make it to Deming in fine shape, won't we, engine? Of course we will. And after Deming is Lordsburg and my goodness we're not far from home at all, are we? You just keep right on chugging along up there, my friend. Chugging right on along.

Comes Deming, sliding by, and once again a road to follow. And Lordsburg. The engine utters no complaint. After Lordsburg I fly off my map into Arizona. But if I follow the road, it will surely lead to Tucson. I sit in the cockpit and watched the powdered ground reel by. The mountains are surprises now, without a map, as if this were all unexplored territory. The next chart I have is for Tucson.

[134]

The road winds for a moment, twisting through the rocky hills. An adobe house to the right, a cluster of mountain buildings to the left, guarding a lake as smooth as engine oil. There is not the faintest ripple of wind.

One certainly becomes impatient when one doesn't know just where one is. Come along, Tucson. Around this curve? This? All right, Tucson . . . let's go, let's go.

We snake down a lonely valley, echoes rebounding from its hills. In Tucson we shall have to look around; big airports and big airplanes there. It will be nice to see another airplane. Why, I haven't seen another airplane since Alabama! Even over Dallas, not a single airplane. Talk about the crowded sky. But perhaps the first thousand feet doesn't count as sky.

And there it is ahead, suddenly, as in the motion pictures of the sailing boats when the lookout shouts land ho and the camera turns to find land only a hundred yards away. There, a silver gleam in the air, an airplane flying. It is a transport making his landing approach to Tucson International. A transport. He looks as foreign in the sky as though he were an oil painting of an airplane, sliding on invisible tracks toward the runway.

To the right is the giant that is Davis-Monthan Air Force Base, with a runway nearly three miles long. I could land on the width of that runway with room to spare, but the mountain-heavy airplanes that fly from the base sometimes need every foot of the length to get off the ground. What a way to fly.

Right there, by the corner where the parking ramp turns, I stood on a weekend alone, with a fighter plane that would not start. Something wrong with the ignition. I could get all kinds of fuel into the burner cans and the tailpipe, but it wouldn't light. . . . I couldn't make it burn. I gravely considered throwing a newspaper afire up that tailpipe, then running around to the cockpit and opening the throttle to spray it with fuel. But a mechanic happened along and fixed the ignition system before I found a newspaper and a match. I can't help but wonder what would have happened.

One other airplane, a little one, in the sky below me, and I rock my wings to him. He doesn't notice. Or he may have noticed, but is one who doesn't believe in wing-rocked greetings between airplanes. That is a custom going out of style, I think, wing-rocking to say hello and don't-worry-I-see-you. Well, I'll give it a chance to live on, anyway. Sort of a comradely thing to do, I think, and I might be able to set the custom going again; have everyone rocking their wings to everyone else. Jet transports, bombers, lightplanes, business planes. Hm. That might be carrying it a little far. Perhaps it's best that only a few keep the custom going.

One mountain north of Tucson and it is time to land once more, at an ex-Army field. Marana Air Park, they call it now. Like planting flowers in a hand grenade. Hard surface here, and straight into the wind. I should be getting used to the biplane by now, but there is that strange wall of hurry between us. We land without incident, and stop. Yet there is a moment in which I know that I could not control the airplane if it veered to left or right, as though we were sliding on buttered glass. Something is gone. My rushing, my placing California before learning has breached the trust between us, and the biplane has not stopped to teach or even to imply a lesson since before the thunderstorm. She has been cold and void of life, she has been a machine only. Watching the familiar fuel pour into the familiar tank, I wish that I could slow down, could take my time. But the closer I come to home, the harder I drive the biplane and myself. I am helpless, I am swept up in a windstorm of hurry and nothing matters except getting home tomorrow.

# 1 3

THE MAGNETO AGAIN. Only ten minutes after takeoff, the left mag is misfiring. Clearly it is not Automatic Rough at work, for below is Casa Grande and an airport into the wind. It is just that the engine is misfiring and backfiring whenever the left magneto is called upon to spark the cylinders by itself. The right mag works well, with only an occasional single missing of a single beat. Decision time once again, and more difficult. Land now at a field that has some limited repair facilities and find the trouble, or continue on, using the right mag alone?

No answer from the airplane, as if she is sitting back and watching me dispassionately, not caring whether the decision I make here means safety or destruction. If only I were not in a hurry to be home. It would be prudent to stop. Prudence and I haven't been getting along too well these last days, but

[137]

after all, one should sometimes follow its leadings.

All the while, Casa Grande drifts slowly behind. I don't have much money, and it would cost money even if the little hangar there would have the parts the engine needs. If I go ahead, I'm gambling that the good magneto will stay good across the next three hundred miles of desert. If I lose, I'll land on the highway and seek the help of my fellow man. That's not too bad a fate, or a very high penalty to pay. What does an airplane engine have two magnetos for, anyway? So that it can run all day on one magneto, it can run all its life on one magneto. Decision made. We go on.

With the decision, a wind rising out of the west. A time for patience has once again arrived, and at altitude, in the midst of the wind, I am slowed so that a lone automobile, towing a house trailer, keeps in perfect pace with me. The cost of my decision to fly with an ailing ignition system is that I fly at altitude and do not allow myself the trick of flying close to the ground in avoidance of the wind. My only negotiable asset now is altitude and I cannot afford to squander it for a few miles per hour. At least I am moving westward.

I'm not concerned, and engine failure is an academic sort of problem from Casa Grande to Yuma, for this is land that I know well and that I have seen day after day and month after month. Just on the other side of those same Santan Mountains off my right wing lies Williams Air Force Base. Just after I had finally earned the right to wear the wings of an Air Force pilot, I came to this land, and to the magnificent swift airplane that was numbered F-86F and that was coded *Sabrejet*. From those runways we flew, nervous at first in a single-seat airplane in which the first time we flew, we flew alone. And it was such a simple airplane to fly that we would finish our short before-takeoff checklist there on the concrete and stop and wait and shake our heads and mutter, certain that we had forgotten something. You mean all you do is push this little handle forward and let go of the brakes and then *fly?* That's what they meant, and following that opening routine we came up from those runways to cross this same desert.

To my left are a few hundred square miles marked Restricted Area on my map, and that are indeed restricted, as far as biplanes are concerned. But then Restricted meant Our Very Own, where we flew to find the strafing targets set in cleared squares of desert and the bull's-eye rings of the bomb circles. But best of all for us was the desolate land called the Applied Tactics Range. Applied Tactics gives the student the feel of what close air support really is. There on the desert are convoys of old rusting automobiles and trucks, are tanks waiting in the sage and yucca, are roundhouses and artillery emplacements. Once in a while we would be allowed to practice combat tactics on these, learning such basic tenets as Never Strafe a Convoy Lengthwise; Never Attack Twice from the Same Direction; Concentrate Your Fire.

Maybe they're out there today. If I could make it very quiet, maybe I could hear the sound of the engines and the thud of the practice rockets hitting the sand and the popcorn sound of the fifty-caliber machine guns firing. This is happy country, from a time of good days, filled with that rare sort of friend that one only finds when adventure is shared, and when one trusts one's life to another.

Where are they in this twist of now? Those other pilots are no longer about me every day, briefing for the first flight before the sun has risen. Some who flew this land with me are still flying, some are not. Some are the same, some have changed. One a purchasing agent now for a giant corporation, one a warehouse manager, one an airline pilot, one in the Air Force, a career man. The friend within them is driven hard in a corner, by trivial things. Talk not to him of rent or taxes or

[139]

how the home team is doing. The friend within is found in action, in the important things of flying smoothly in the weather, in calling the fuel check, the oxygen check, and in trying to put more bulletholes in the target than any other friend can do.

It is strange to discover this. Here is the same man, that same body whose voice came once on the radio saying, Look at that, and I'd turn and look over my right wing and there would be an isolated mountaintop in spring, with its base all brown and dry, and from its razor top the wind pulling a white tatter of snow, absolutely without sound, and alone. The quiet wind on a quiet mountaintop, and the trail of snow like spray from a mid-ocean stormwave. And in "look at that" a friend is revealed. There is no triviality in those words. They are to say, Notice our mortal enemy, the mountain. He can at times be so very cruel, yet at times like these he can be very handsome, too, can he not? You've got to have respect for a mountain.

Without mountains over which to be concerned, the friend shrinks away. When the purchase order and the desk become the important things in a life, the friend is difficult to reach. One can break through, of course, with sheer power and anguish and see again for a second or two the friend within. Hey! Bo! Remember the day when I was dialing a radio in my cockpit and you were flying my wing and you touched your microphone and said, Plan on flying into that hill, ace? Don't you remember that?

A stirring within, and an answer from the friend.

I remember; don't worry. I remember. Those days were bright, but we can never live them again, can we? Why must we hurt ourselves in the remembering?

There is a shock of cold when I realize that the desk mind

has taken over so much of the thought of a friend and that his brilliant life has become a calm plain. No more the roaring laughing highs of pulling contrails in the sun or rolling down into an attack. No more the furious caged lows of being caught for days on the ground by fog that doesn't show the other side of the flight line. Nothing devastating ever happens to a purchasing agent, and nothing filled with delight.

The Restricted Area falls away behind and with it a few lumps of crusted lead, copper clad, buried in the sand, that once shimmered from my gun barrels. Ahead, another mountain, and a town called Yuma. Almost home country, now, biplane. Almost there. But it is surprising how big even home country can be. And for a reason unknown a fragment of statistic drifts through my mind. The great majority of all aircraft crashes occur within twenty-five miles of an airplane's home base. One of those undoubtedly meaningless things, but of the sort that is so cunningly worded that one remembers it.

Easy to chase that foreboding. I'm not within twenty-five miles of my home base. I'm a lot closer to it than I was a few sunrises ago, but it is still over the horizon ahead.

With the Colorado River below and California air whistling about me, I have the courage to try the other magneto. And now, after two hours running on the right magneto, the left one works perfectly. The last time I tried it, at Casa Grande, backfires and puffs of black smoke from the exhaust. Now, smooth as the youngest of kittens. What a most unusual engine.

Biplane, we are almost home. Hear that? A little more desert to do, one more stop for gasoline, and you'll be in a warm hangar once again. The Salton Sea glimmers ahead and the squares of green-blotter land to the south of it. Anything can happen now and we can say we have made it to California.

Still, it is a California just in name and feels like home only as Saturday feels like Saturday because I've seen a calendar. This desert, and the baked blotter land doesn't shout, *California!* the way the long beaches do, or smooth golden hills or the sudden mass of the Sierra Nevada. One isn't truly in California until one is west of those mountains.

The biplane's wings flick suddenly dull, as if a switch were thrown. Surprised, we have been enveloped in dusk. The switch is the Sierra itself, thrown to block the sun, casting a giant dark knife-shadow across the desert. The familiar first-lights of cautious automobiles sparkle on the road toward Palm Springs, hurrying in for the night. Our night will be Palm Springs, too, nested down in the grey blur at the base of San Jacinto Mountain. There is now the turning greenflash whiteflash of the airport beacon. And there, spilling over the top of a peak marked on my chart as 10,804 feet above sea level, clouds, as black as the mountain itself.

Palm Springs, airplane! Home of motion-picture stars and heads of state and giants of enterprise. Better, Palm Springs is less than a day from your own home, a hangar again, and Sunday-afternoon flights. Like that, airplane?

There is no response from the Parks. As we turn to land, not the faintest hint of reply.

# 14

THE AIRPORT AT PALM SPRINGS is a rather exclusive place and parked upon it are the most elite and the most expensive airplanes in the world. There is this morning, however, something radically wrong. At the very end of a long row of polished twin-engine aircraft, in fact parked almost in the sagebrush, is a strange oily old biplane. It is tied to the ground by a rope at each wingtip and one at the tail. Underneath the wing, as the grey sun rises, is a dim sleeping bag stretched on the cool concrete.

It is raining. Once a year in Palm Springs it rains, and in the worst years twice. What instrument of coincidence has timed my arrival with the arrival of the Day of Rain? There are no other sleeping bags spread on the concrete of the airport and I must consider this alone.

The rain is light at first, from broken clouds. At first, too,

the wetness makes merely the background for a white silhouette in dry of the biplane, and I lie along the dry left wing of the silhouette. The rain goes on, drumming first on the top wing, then slowly falling in big drops from the top wing to boom against the fabric of the lower wing. A pretty sound, and I lie unconcerned and listen. Mount San Jacinto scowls down at me, clouds spraying over its towering peak. I'll cross you today, San Jacinto, and then it is all downhill to home. Two hours' flying from here at most, and I shall discover what it feels like to sleep once again in a bed.

The rain continues, and the wetness takes on a sheen of tiny depth. Lying now with my head on the concrete and with my lowest eye open, I can see a wall of water advancing, fully a sixteenth of an inch high. This is a great deal of rain, and the drumming and booming on my wing should stop any second now.

It doesn't. The wall of water advances slowly into my dry sanctuary. The thirsty concrete drinks, but to no avail. New drops still rush to reinforce the water. By tiny leaps and minuscule bounds, the wall advances. If I were less than a millimeter tall, it would be an awesome spectacle of rampaging nature. Pinpoint twigs and branches are being swept up into that wall, waves thereon are foaming and cresting and the roar of their advance can be heard for inches around. A fearsome, terrifying sight, that water rushing, sweeping over everything in its path. The only reason that I do not run screaming before it is a matter of perspective, an ability to make myself so big that the water is nothing, and of no danger. And I wonder as I watch. Can it be the same with all fearsome things? Can we lift ourselves so far above them that their terror is lost? I wonder, and for the briefest part of a second I can swear that I sense a faint, tired smile. Perhaps my friend is awake once again, briefly returned to lesson teaching.

Phase II of the Lesson of the Advancing Water is that, no matter the perspective, one cannot ignore the problem. Even though it is suddenly only a barely moving film of moisture and not a flash flood of the desert, it can still be annoying and uncomfortable unless I soon solve the problem. My silhouette of dryness grows narrower as the rain continues, and unless I find some way to stop the water's advance or decide that wet sleeping bags aren't so bad after all, I'll be forced to flee.

Unshaven, oil-covered, disheveled with the worst of the barnstormers, I gather my sleeping bag and race for shelter in the luxurious office and waiting room of the general-aviation terminal. Would a good barnstormer have gotten wet? I wonder as I run through the rain. No. A good barnstormer would have climbed into the cockpit, under the waterproof cover, and have been asleep again in an instant. Ah, well. It takes time to learn.

Against one wall of the deserted room is a telephone, a direct line to the weather bureau. It is a strange feeling to hold a telephone in my hand again. A voice comes from the thing, with an offer of general aid.

"I'm at Palm Springs. Want to get across into Long Beach /Los Angeles. How does it look through the pass?" I should have said The Pass. Almost every pilot who flies to Southern California has flown through the gigantic slot cut between the mountains San Jacinto and San Gorgonio. On a windy day, one can count on being tossed about in the pass, but so many new pilots have exaggerated its rigors that even old pilots are beginning to believe that it is a dangerous place.

"The pass is closed."

Why is it that weathermen are so smug when the weather is bad? At last they can put the pilots in their places? The arrogant devils need to be set back a notch, now and then? "Banning has a two-hundred-foot overcast with one-mile

[146]

visibility in rain; probably won't get much better all day long."

The devil it won't. The chances of that weather staying so bad all day are about the same as the chances of Palm Springs being flooded in the next half hour.

"How about the pass at Borego or Julian, or San Diego?"

"We don't have any weather for the passes themselves. San Diego is calling three thousand overcast and light rain."

I'll just have to try them and see.

"How's the Los Angeles weather?"

"Los Angeles . . . let's see . . . Los Angeles is calling fifteen hundred broken to overcast, light rain. Forecast to remain the same all day. A pilot report has the pass closed, by the way, and severe turbulence."

"Thanks."

He catches me before I hang up, with a request for my airplane number. Always the entries to make in his logs, and no doubt for a very good reason.

Once I get on the other side of the mountains, there will be no problem. The weather is not quite clear, but it is good enough for finding one's way about. Banning is in the middle of the pass, and the weather it is reporting is not good. But the report may be hours old. I can't expect much so early in the morning, but I might as well give Banning a try before I run down along the mountain chain, poking my nose into every pass for a hundred miles. One of them is sure to be open.

Twenty minutes later the biplane and I round the corner of San Jacinto and head into the pass. It certainly does not look good. As if someone has made a temporary bedroom out of Southern California, and has hung a dirty grey blanket between it and the desert, for privacy. If I can make it to Banning, I can stop and wait for the weather to lift.

Below, the highway traffic goes unconcernedly ahead, al-

[147]

though the road is slick and shiny in rain. A few drops of rain smear the front windscreen of the biplane, a few more. I have my spot all picked to land if the engine stops in the rain, but it doesn't falter. Perhaps the biplane, too, is in a hurry. The rain pours down and I discover that one doesn't get wet flying rainstorms in an open cockpit airplane. The last rainstorm I flew into, I hadn't noticed. The rain doesn't really fall, but blows at me head on, and the windscreen kicks it up and over my head. If I want to get wet, I have to stick my head around to one side of the glass panels.

Funny. It doesn't feel as if I'm getting wet at all. The rain feels like rice, good and dry, thrown a hundred miles an hour into my face. It is only when my head is back in the cockpit and when I feel my helmet with an ungloved hand that I find it wet. The rain gets goggles sparkling clean.

After a few minutes of rain, the first turbulence hits. Often I have heard turbulence described as a giant fist smashing down upon an airplane. I have never really felt it that way in a small airplane until this second. The fist is just the size of a biplane, and it is swinging down at the end of a very long arm. It strikes the airplane so hard that I am thrown against the safety belt and have to hold tightly to the control stick to keep my hand from being jerked away. Strange air, this. Not the constant slamming of the twisted roiled air that one expects from winds across rocky places, but smooth . . . smooth, and BAM! Then smooth . . . smooth . . . BAM! The rain grows heavier, in great weeping veils sorrowing down to the ground. The sky is solid water ahead. We can't get through.

We turn away, not really discouraged, for we hadn't expected to get through the first thing in the morning.

Whenever I turn away from bad weather in an airplane not equipped to fly by instruments, I feel very self-righteous. The proper thing to do. The number one cause of fatal accidents in light aircraft, the statistics say, is the pilot who tries to push the weather, to slip through without going on instruments. I'll push the weather with the best of 'em, I say sanctimoniously, but I'll always do it with a path open behind me. The biplane, with its instruments that give only a rough approximation of altitude and a misty vague idea of heading, on a wobbly compass, is not built to fly through any weather. Any weather at all. If I absolutely had to, I might be able to get it down through an overcast, flying with my hands off the stick and holding perhaps the W in the compass by rudder alone. But that's a last-ditch effort, taken only where the land below is flat and I know for sure that the ceiling is at least one thousand feet.

There are those who say that you can spin down through an overcast, and I'd agree with them; a good procedure. But I have heard that with a few of the old airplanes the spin turns into a flat spin after three or four revolutions, and from a flat spin there is no recourse save the parachute. This may be one of the rumors, and untrue. But the danger therein is my thought, I do not *know*. Not the flat spin, but the fear of the flat spin keeps me from an otherwise practical and effective emergency procedure. It is much easier to stay away from the weather.

The first round goes to San Jacinto, and taking its strange knocking about, we fly, filled with righteousness, back out of the pass. What a fine example we are setting for all the younger pilots. Here is a pilot who has flown instruments before and often, for hours and in thick cloud, turning back from a bit of mist that obscures the ground. What a fine example am I. How much the prudent pilot. I shall live to be very old. Unfortunately, no one is watching.

We turn south along the eastern edge of the mountains,

[149]

over the bright green squares in the sand that irrigation has wrought. And we climb. It takes a long time to gain altitude. Playing the thermals and the upslope winds as hard as I can, I rise only to the level of the lower peaks; a little more than eight thousand feet, where it is freezing once again. At least here, when I can no longer stand the cold, I have only to come down a little to be warm once again.

We won't even try Borego Pass. A long narrow gorge running diagonally through the mountains, it is walled only a short way down its length by the same blanket of grey that covers the pass at San Jacinto.

South some more and third time must be the charm. More rough, high country, but at least the cloud is not so bad. I turn at Julian toward a narrow gap in the mountain, and follow a winding road.

The wind through the gap is a direct headwind as I fly west. It flattens the grass along the roadside and the road's white line creeps reluctantly past my wing. It must be blowing fifty miles an hour at this altitude. There is an awesomeness about it, an uneasy feeling that I am not wanted here, as if I am being lured into the gap in order that some hungry dragon within can have his fill of warm engine and crushed wingspars. We fly and fly and struggle and fly against the wind, and finally the gap is ours. We are through, to a land of high valleys and peaceful green farms in mountain meadows. But look down there. The grass, even the short grass, is being flattened silver by the wind, it is being ironed onto the ground by it. That wind must be fifty miles per hour now at the *surface!*

This is work, and not fun at all. If the wind would only be on my tail, it would be fun. Ahead, the clouds, watching me and grinning maliciously. The only way out of the valley ahead is to follow the road, and the cloud turns into fog that lies on the road like a big fuzzy barbell that can never be lifted. It is sad. We have fought so hard to get here. Perhaps we can land. If we land here, surely we can outwait the clouds and continue westward this afternoon. The meadows look very good for landing. Light rain in the air, but much sun too. Suddenly they combine off the right wing into a brilliant full-circle rainbow, a really bright one, almost opaque in its radiance. Normally the rainbow would be a beautiful sight, worthy of awe, but I still must fight to move an inch against the wind and I can only take snapshots with my eyes and hope that later, when I am not fighting, I'll be able to remember the rainbow for what it is, and as fresh and as bright as it is.

I shall land, and save the advance I've made. So, decision made, down comes the little biplane from its rainbow, toward the wet green grass of the meadow. A good landing place ahead, worth inspecting closely. Grass is taller than it looked. And wet. Probably a lot of mud under that grass, and these are hard narrow high-pressure tires, perfect for bogging up to axles in. Look there: a cow. I've heard of cows eating the fabric right off old airplanes. Something in the dope that they like.

So much for that meadow.

Near a farmhouse, another field to check. Except for the trees, it looks soft and smooth. Should be able to hover right in over the top of them. But what would happen if the wind stops? I'd never be able to get out again. Remember, this valley is four thousand feet high, and that's some pretty thin air. Only way I'd ever get off again would be in this hurricane wind. Hot day, or no wind, and I'd need four times as much room to get into the air at all. Two fields, two vetos. One more chance, anyway; maybe the pass to San Diego is open, down by the Mexican border.

Landing forgotten, we turn the headwind into tailwind and shoot from the high valleys of Julian like a wheat puff from a cereal gun.

Being cuffed about like a toy glider has a wearing effect on one's nerves. Last chance, coming up. San Diego. South again across more miles of desert, thinking of nothing but how lonely it would be to have to land here, and how much land we really have in this country that we do not use. Think of all the houses that could be put on this one little stretch of desert. Now all we have to do is coax somebody to come out and live here.

One last highway, the one that leads to San Diego. I have only to fly along this road, as though I were an automobile, and I shall get to San Diego; from there an easy matter to fly up the beach to home. I am an automobile. I am an automobile.

We bank and follow the road. The wind is a living thing, and it doesn't like the biplane at all. It punches at us constantly, it jabs and batters as if there is an urgent need for it to perfect its style and its rhythm. I hold to the stick very tightly. We must be making progress, but the hilltop to our left is certainly not moving very quickly. It has been there for two minutes. I check the road.

Oh, merciful heavens. We're moving backward! It is a dizzying feeling, and the first time I have ever seen it from the cockpit of an airplane. I have to steady myself and hold even more tightly to the stick. An airplane must move through the air in order to fly, and almost always that means that it moves over the ground, too. But now white lines in the road are passing me, and I have the strange feeling that I had over Odessa, that I have when I stand at the top of a ladder or a tall building and look down. As if there is a tremendous fall coming in the next few seconds. The airspeed needle is firm on 80 miles per hour. The wind must be at least 85 mph on my nose. The biplane simply cannot move to the west. Nothing I can do will make her move in the direction of the Pacific Ocean.

This is getting ridiculous. We bank hard to the right, dive away from the wind, and I can pluck one single straw of consolation from seeing the highway scream past as I turn east. With the tailwind, my groundspeed must be 180 miles per hour. If I could only hold it, I could set a new biplane speed record to North Carolina. But I am wiser than to really believe that the wind will hold, and I know that just before I cross the South Carolina border into North Carolina the wind would shift to become an eighty-mile headwind, and I would hang suspended in the air one hundred yards from the finish line, unable to reach it. This is a wonderful day for playing all kinds of improbable games with an airplane. I can land the biplane backward today and take off straight up. I can fly sideways across the ground, in fact be more maneuverable than a helicopter could be. But I do not feel like playing games. I only want to accomplish what should be the simple task of reaching the other side of these mountains. Possibly I could tack back and forth, a sailboat in the sky, and eventually reach San Diego. No. Tacking is a meek and subservient thing to do, not befitting the character of an airplane. One must draw the line somewhere.

The only fitting technique is to fight the mountains for every inch I gain, and if the mountains for a moment prove the stronger, to retire, and rest and turn and fight again. For, when the fight belongs to the mountain, it is not proper to seek sly and devious means of sneaking around its might.

There is no mistaking the rebuff of the lesser mountain passes. They are making it clear that my adversary shall be the giant San Jacinto, ruling the pass into Banning.

I have burned a full tank of fuel in the fight to get across the mountains, and have gotten nowhere. Or, more precisely, I have gotten to Borego Springs Airport, one hard runway standing alone in the sagebrush and clouds of dust. Circling overhead, I see that the windsock is standing straight out, across the runway. In a moment it gusts around to point down the asphalt strip, and in another second it is cross again. To land on that runway in the gusting changing high-velocity wind will be to murder one biplane. Yet I must land, and haven't the fuel to reach for Palm Springs again. I shall land in the desert near the Borego Airport.

An inspection of the dry land rules that out. The surface is just too rough. Catch the wheels in a steep sand dune and we'll be on our back in less than a second, and only with incredible luck could we escape with less than forty broken wingribs, a bent propeller and an engine full of sand and sagebrush. So much for landing in the desert.

The infield of the airport itself is dirt and sand, dotted with huge sage. I turn the biplane down through the shuddering wind and fly over the windsock, watching the infield. It was level, once. The bulldozers must have leveled it when they scraped a bed for the runway. The brush is three feet high over it, four feet, some places. I could land in the brush, dead slow in the wind, and hope there aren't any pipes or ditches in the ground. If there are, it will be worse than the open desert. We fly two more passes, inspecting the brush, trying to see the ground beneath it.

At the gas pump, a man stands and watches, a small figure in blue coveralls. What a gulf lies between us! He is as safe and content as he can be, he can even go to sleep leaning against the gas pump, if he wants. But a thousand feet, a hundred feet away, the Parks and I are in trouble. My cork-and-wire fuel gage shows that the tank is empty. We got

[154]

ourselves into this affair and we've got to get ourselves out. The wind gusts at a wide angle to the runway, and a brush landing is the least of our evils. With luck, we will emerge with a few minor scratches.

One last climb for a few hundred feet of working altitude, throttle back, turn into the wind and drop toward the brush. Should the wind shift now, we shall need more than luck.

The Parks settles like a snail in a bright-colored parachute, barely moving across the ground. The brush is tall and brown beneath us, and I fight to keep from pushing the throttle and bolting safely back into the sky. As we scrape the tops of the sage, it is clear that we are not moving slowly at all. Hard back on the stick, hold tight to the throttle and in a crash and rumbling clatter we plow into a waist-high sea of blurred and brittle twigs. There is a snapping all about us, like a forest fire running wild, and twigs erupt in a whirling fountain from the propeller, spraying in a high arc to spin over the top wing and rain into the cockpit. The lower wing cuts like a scythe through the stuff, shredding it, tumbling it in a wide straight swath behind. And we are stopped, after breaking our way almost to the edge of the asphalt, all in one dusty piece, trembling in the wind, still throwing fresh-snapped twigs from the propeller. Throttle forward, we grimly crush ahead to the runway, turn to slowly follow a taxiway leading toward the gas pump.

"That was quite a landing you made, there." The man hands up the hose, and searches for the sixty-weight oil.

"Make 'em that way all the time."

"Wasn't quite sure just what you were doing. Can't remember anybody ever landing out in the brush like that. That's kind of hard on the airplane, isn't it?"

"She's built for it."

"Guess you'll be staying the night, in this wind?"

[155]

"No. You got a candy machine around, peanuts or something?"

"Yeah, we got a candy machine. You say you won't be staying?"

"No."

"Where you headed?"

"Los Angeles."

"Kind of a long way, isn't it? A hundred miles? I mean for an old biplane like this?"

"You are right, there. One hundred miles is a long, long way."

But I am not dismayed, and as I pull the *Peanuts* selector handle, the oily image in the mirror is smiling.

# 1 5

IN FIFTEEN MINUTES WE ARE AIRBORNE again, slamming through the whitecaps in the air, beating north across the wind. The safety belt is strained down tight, and the silver nose is pointed toward the shrouded peak of San Jacinto.

All right, mountain, this is it. I can do without my self-righteousness now. I'll fight you all day long if I have to, to reach that runway at Banning. Today there will be no waiting for the weather to clear. I will fight you until the fuel tank is empty again, then fill the tank and come back and fight you for another five hours. But I tell you, mountain, I am going to make it through that pass today.

San Jacinto does not appear to be awed by my words. I feel like a knight, lance leveled, plumes flying, galloping at The Pass. It is a long gallop, and by the time I arrive at the tournament grounds we have used an hour of fuel. Plenty of

fuel left to fly to Banning, and to spare. Come along, my little steed. First the lance, then the mace, then the broadsword.

The mountain's mace hits us first, and it slams us down so hard that the fuel is jerked from the carburetor, the engine stops for a full second and my hand is ripped from the control stick. Then calm again.

San Jacinto is inscrutable, covered in its Olympian mist. Quite some mace it swings. Lance broken, it is time for my broadsword.

Another impossibly hard crash of air upon us, the engine stops for the count of two and I clutch the control stick with both hands. We are sheathed again in rainwater and raindrops whip back over my head like buckshot. We don't scare, mountain. We'll make Banning if we have to taxi there on the highway.

In reply, another smash of the mace, as if the mountain needs the time between blows to swing the spinning iron thing high over its head, to get the more power. In the force of it, I am fired against my safety belt, my boots are thrown from the rudder pedals, the world blurs as my head snaps back. And still Banning is not in sight. Airplane, can you take any more of this? I am asking much of you today, and I have not inspected your spars and fittings.

I can take it if you can, pilot.

The words smash into my mind as though the mace had driven them there. My airplane is back! It is a strange and wonder-filled time. A glorious time. I am no longer fighting alone, but fighting with my airplane. And in the middle of a fight, a lesson. As long as the pilot can believe in his fight, and battle on, his airplane will battle with him. When he believes his airplane has failed him, or will soon fail, he opens the door to disaster. If you don't trust an airplane, you can never be a pilot.

[159]

Another mace, and I can hear it hit the biplane. Above the wind, above the engine and the rain, the hard WHAM of an incredible blow.

But ahead, now, ahead! Lying low in the rain, a shiny slick runway. In white letters across the end of it, BANNING. Come on, my little friend, we have almost won. Two strikes of the mace in quick succession, loud strikes that pitch us almost inverted, and I would not be surprised to hear spars snapping with the next blow. But I must trust the airplane. I lost my broadsword long ago, and we fight now with our bare hands. Only another minute . . .

And Banning is ours. We can turn now and land and rest.

But again, look ahead. The clouds have lifted, ever so slightly. I can see light between a foothill of the mountain and the cloud. Fly through that crack and the fight is over, I'm sure the fight will be over.

Banning fades slowly into the rain behind us.

This is a foolhardy thing to do. We could have stayed at the airport until this all lifted clear. You won your fight, you could have gloated over that piece of ill judgment without adding another to it. If that crack closes now ahead of you, where would you go, with Banning lost behind? Ninety percent of the crashes, they say, within twenty-five miles of home base.

Quiet, caution. I'll land in the fields down there and in this wind I won't roll very far. Now be quiet.

It is quiet from the dissenter's gallery for the moment, the quiet of someone phrasing in his mind the most vengeful way of saying I told you so.

The mace is not hitting us squarely any more and the engine no longer stops in the force of it. We are one mile from the opening between cloud and ground over the hill. If it stays open for another minute and a half, we'll be through. There will be perhaps a thirty-foot clearance. A mace blow glancing, smashing the biplane into a wild right bank.

Recovering, wheels swishing the top of the hill, we squeak through the crack, and instantly fly out of the dark rain. Instantly, in the blink of an eye. Whoever has been directing the action for this flight has been doing a magnificent job, so good that no one save a pilot will believe the land spread out before us as we cross the hill.

The clouds ahead are broken, and through them the golden shafts of sunlight pierce down like bright javelins thrown into the earth. A bit of an old hymn is tossed into my thought: ". . . from mist and shadow into Truth's clear day."

The day has color again. Sunlight. I have not known what sunlight means until this moment. It brings life and brilliant things to the air and to the ground under the air. It is bright. It is warm. It turns the dirt into emerald and lakes into the deep clear blue of a washed sky. It makes clouds so white that you have to squint even behind your dark goggles.

If the people working in the green fields below could have listened very carefully, they would have heard, high in the eucalyptus-wind, mixed with engine noise from that little red-and-yellow biplane, a tiny voice singing. I no longer have to hurry.

The first buildings of Los Angeles and its thousand suburbs slide beneath us, and from habit we climb. No chance of being lonely if we must land now. Stop the engine this moment and we shall land on the city golf course. This, and it's the parking lot at Disneyland, big enough to land transports on. This, and we have the engineered concrete bed of the Los Angeles river.

But in no moment does the engine stop, as if the biplane is eager to see her new home and hangar, and has no patience

for failures. "You can't go wrong with a Wright," the barn-stormers used to say, and so it has proved. After playing its few harmless practical jokes, the Whirlwind engine has laughed at us and shows now the truth of the saying. We haven't gone wrong.

We turn one last time, to enter a busy traffic pattern. One last runway tilting beneath us, rising out of the city. Compton Airport. Home. We have come twenty-seven hundred miles across a country, and now, oil trailing back from our silver cowl, wet dust spraying from beneath our tall wheels, past fitting smoothly into present, our journey is done. We have been splintered across runways; frozen in midair; blasted in flying sand; soaked in rain; beaten in mountain winds; scourged in brittle sage; we have flickered back and forth through the years, a brightwinged bird in time, and we have arrived home. Has the arriving been worth the travail of the journey? A good question. I rather doubt that a biplane cross-country craze will soon be sweeping the nation.

We wheel slowly into a hangar and rumble its giant heavy door closed against the busy modern sounds of a busy modern time.

In the miles and sand and rain and years, we have learned only a little about ourselves, picked up just a tiny fraction of knowing about one man and one old biplane, and about what they mean to each other. At the last, in the sudden quiet of a dark hangar, man and biplane alone together, we find our answer to the question of the journey. Four words.

It was worth it.